THE SCHOOL OF PARIS

THE SCHOOL
OF PARIS

IN THE

MUSÉE D'ART MODERNE

BERNARD DORIVAL

Curator, Musée National d'Art Moderne, Paris

HARRY N. ABRAMS, INC., PUBLISHERS, NEW YORK

TRANSLATED FROM THE FRENCH BY
CORNELIA BROOKFIELD AND ELLEN HART

LIBRARY OF CONGRESS CATALOG CARD NUMBER: 62—14853
1962
PRINTED IN WEST GERMANY BY CARL SCHÜNEMANN
THIS BOOK IS PUBLISHED IN FRANCE BY
EDITIONS AIMERY SOMOGY, PARIS

CONTENTS

ORIGINS OF THE SCHOOL OF PARIS

Three times, at least, in the course of a long history, France, and particularly Paris, has experienced a supreme flowering of art. The first was the period we call Gothic – following the Italians of the Renaissance for whom the word had a pejorative meaning. The men of the twelfth and thirteenth centuries on the other hand, called it 'opus francigenum'. This art made its influence felt across the whole extent of Western Christendom from Spain to Scandinavia, from Scotland to Poland and even as far as the distant 'marches' of Cyprus, Rhodes, Syria and Palestine. The next period lasted during the century and a half when princes, kings, even emperors and empresses – Stanislas Poniatowski, Frederick the Great, Maria Theresa and Catherine the Great of Russia – looked to Versailles and Paris and dreamed of adopting the ways and customs, the fashions and the arts in vogue 'at the Court and in the City' – those of Louis XIV, Louis XV and Louis XVI. Finally, it is the last century that has perhaps seen the zenith of this artistic brilliance of Paris.

True, the prestige of Paris had been at a peak during the era of the last of the Capets and the first of the Valois – who were emulated by the sovereigns of Europe, especially the emperors of the House of Luxembourg, with their chief seat in Prague, – but from the twelfth to the fourteenth century other centres, the great abbeys like Cîteaux, and cities such as the Avignon of the Popes, contended with the royal capital for leadership in the arts. Further, from 1660 to 1789, the focus was not so much Paris as Versailles, so that European art took its directions from the one as much as the other. However, from about 1850, Paris has had no rival in France, and when we see the art of France as the paramount influence, this is the art of Paris alone.

This influence has been marked during the last hundred years, just as in earlier periods, by a two-way movement – French artists have gone to live and work abroad, and there has been an influx of foreign artists into Paris. So it was that the architect of the cathedral of Toledo may have been the same who designed the cathedral of Bourges, and the most imposing of the Gothic structures of the Near East were the work of French master-builders. Three or four centuries later, we find the European Courts swarming with architects, sculptors and painters from France, and Catherine the Great approaching Falconet to make a statue of Peter the Great. And then there was the State Parliament of Virginia going to Houdon for a statue of Washington. In the same way today, a host of artists born in France or settled there are to be found working all over the world, their canvases filling the galleries and private collections of Europe, America and even Japan.

More striking than the centrifugal force that takes a Matisse to Moscow or to Merion [1], a Léger to New York, a Le Corbusier to Srinagar and Tokyo, is the movement in the opposite direction which draws a flood of artists to the banks of the Seine, artists – and more especially painters – of every tongue, race and civilization. It is perfectly true that the Paris of the end of the thirteenth century and beginning of the fourteenth had seen a throng of Flemings, a dazzling company of Italians, crowding into the city enclosed within the walls of Philippe Auguste; and again, the Paris of Boucher and Fragonard welcomed a Lavreince, a Roslin, a Hall and a Heinsius. However, the press of foreigners coming in was never in the past as great as it has been since the middle of the nineteenth century. This phenomenon is easily accounted for by the opening up of the New World, which was becoming Europeanised; the spread of European culture in the Near, Middle and Far East; the improvement of transport and of all forms of communication. Still, we should perhaps add a further explanation: the growing prestige of Paris, which for a hundred years or more has kept the role inherited from Rome at the end of the sixteenth century and the beginning of the seventeenth, as a centre

---

[1] In 1932–3 Matisse painted huge murals, the *Dance*, for the Barnes Foundation at Merion, near Philadelphia, U. S. A.

of experiments in art, and as the place which alone, on the international plane, has set authentic values in art and especially in painting.

The Romantic in painting had had several brilliant centres besides Paris, such as London, Düsseldorf and Rome. It was France, however, who started the quest for theories of painting to take its place. Germany still clung to her fusing of painting with philosophy (to be seen also in the international colony living in that museum-city of Rome in the mid-nineteenth century). France, bolder than the England of the Pre-Raphaelites, felt the need for fresh inspiration, and went to nature and life for it. Thus, from about 1845 to 1860, the Realist movement of Daumier, Millet and Courbet asserted itself, and at the same time, on the outskirts of Paris, along the river Oise and even more at Barbizon, landscape painters made the countryside of the Ile de France famous. Realism had in Courbet a propagandist whose persuasiveness matched his talent, and it awakened art, in Belgium and Germany in particular, from the torpor induced by an excessive deference to the romanticism of the illuminated 'Book of Hours'. Charles de Groux followed on Leys, Leibl on Kaulbach, and they clearly would not have been the painters they were without the examples of Millet and Courbet. The influence of the Barbizon School, to which crowds of foreigners flocked, bore fruit in Tervuren and The Hague, as well as in the far-off new Roumania of Grigorescu and Andreescu.

Then the disturbances of the Second Empire overtook even painting, and Realism gave way to what may be styled, to use Baudelaire's term, the art of 'modernité'. Guys and Manet were its chief exponents – not forgetting Degas, who was still to express its spirit well after the turn of the century. This feeling for movement, for the fleeting, the momentary apparition (Carpeaux produced some of the most remarkable examples of it in sculpture), took hold of a whole galaxy of landscape painters. Amongst these, Jongkind stands out – a Dutchman settled in France, to which he remained more enduringly faithful than that roving American, Whistler, whose art would baffle us without the model of Manet and without the craze for the Japanese – a fashion just then beginning in Paris. These foreign artists, good and bad, were legion: they came to revel in the Paris of Napoleon III, or eventually to put themselves to school beside Manet or Degas, but with little success. Such were Sargent, Sickert, Bottini, de Nittis, Slevogt, Thaulow, and Zorn.

However, Impressionism had already come into existence, with one of its founders the Englishman Sisley. Despite the lack of appreciation in France it spread to other countries, where it fared no better, so watered down and art-school-ridden were the versions of it that came from Liebermann, or Steer, for instance. The public in Berlin and in London, just as in Paris, remained stubbornly indifferent; the artists, on the other hand, grasped the immense range and import of its message and the most intrepid made their way to France to get to know and understand it better, to turn to good account for their own work the contributions of Monet and Pissarro.

At the same time, during the years 1875–85, there were other masters, unfairly neglected today, who also threw off sparks far beyond French frontiers and attracted numbers of young foreigners. I have in mind particularly Puvis de Chavannes, so greatly admired at the time, whom Hodler and Derkinderen were to take as a model.

Some of the French painters also admired him – and perhaps the grandeur of concept and significance of the work of Seurat, and even more of Gauguin, result precisely from their having produced a kind of fusion between the art of Puvis de Chavannes and that of the Impressionists: a painting that was monumental and colourful, decorative and Symbolist. Exactly the same kind of painting was being worked out by Gauguin's close friend Van Gogh; and it was contact with this new form that set the stamp on the two most considerable of the Scandinavian painters at the end of the century, the Dane, Willemsen, and more especially the Norwegian, Munch, whose debt to art in the Paris of the 'nineties has not been properly recognized.

It may perhaps seem rash to speak of the 'School of Paris' at this point. So fundamental a contribution had been made by Van Gogh, (the Van Gogh of Arles, of Saint-Rémy and Auvers-sur-Oise, rather than the Van Gogh of Paris), that all the foreign artists who thronged Montmartre at the end of the nineteenth century tended to receive rather than give, or contributed but little. The interchange, the fusion between the French native genius and the genius of the various foreign countries represented on the Seine by some of their most *avant-garde* artists, was still in the future. During the years 1890–1900 the Dutchmen Meyer de Hahn and Verkade, the Dane Mogens Ballin, the Hungarian Rippl-Ronai, and even the Swiss Vallotton, the most original among them, were devoted followers of the School of Pont-Aven and of the Nabi Group, borrowing from them more than they brought. In the Fauve movement, too, which owed as much to Van Gogh, now dead, as to Gauguin and Cézanne still living, not a trace of any specifically foreign element can be detected. Even the work of the Dutchman Van Dongen was so 'Parisianised' that he later became sought-after as a portrait painter by Paris society. But all this was changed by Cubism, the first truly international art movement, which was to blend the contribution of French genius with that of other countries.

The Cubist movement was international by virtue of the great number of followers it attracted from abroad. While Fauvism, Nabism, Neo-Impressionism, and Impressionism above all, had scarcely any following outside France, foreigners were legion in the phase of Cubism that ran from 1907 to 1914. This had as its originators, besides the Frenchman Braque, the Spaniard Picasso, and included amongst its exponents Spaniards such as Juan Gris, Poles such as Marcoussis, Hungarians such as Reth, and Russians such as Serge Férat, – not to speak of the Dutchman Mondrian, the Mexican Diego Rivera, painters who brought out their first works under its banner. Cubist sculpture, too, was the work of foreign artists, of Spaniards like Gargallo, Russians like Zadkine, Lipchitz and Archipenko, Hungarians like Beothy, and Rumanians like Brancusi. In no artistic movement before had Frenchmen and foreigners worked out a new art form together in such a close, brotherly fashion.

It is not surprising that this new art often has a foreign flavour. To be sure, no painting is more French than Braque's, and in the version of Cubism evolved by Gleizes and by the Villon brothers at Courbevoie and Puteaux, the foreign element shrinks to a very small trace, even to vanishing point. But it was different with the Cubism that was born in the Montmartre studio of Picasso at the Bateau-Lavoir: its magic bewitched Juan Gris and Marcoussis to a point (especially if sculpture be included) where the movement could be described as a pooling of French, Spanish and Slav talents and resources – some more perceptible in one painter and some in another. Picasso can in fact as easily be placed in the line of El Greco and Goya, or Juan Gris in that of Zurbarán, as Braque among the kin of Louis Le Nain, Chardin and Corot. Reciprocal influence is here seen at work, as in the Orphic Cubism of Delaunay and his wife, Sonia Terk.

In this last instance, the mutual influence is not to be wondered at. The Delaunays worked in a union of heart and mind so complete that it is almost impossible to detect which of their Orphic canvases is by the one, which by the other. The colourist tradition inherited from Delacroix and Cézanne is here united with the native Russian taste for vivid and gaudy colours, so closely that one can understand why this art, at once French and foreign, should have so easily captivated foreigners, – those who worked in Paris like the Americans Bruce and Wright, or those in Munich, where Franz Marc, August Macke and the young Paul Klee owed as much to the Delaunays as to the Germanised Russian, Kandinsky.

Like Orphic Cubism, abstract art, which had its beginnings in Paris as well as in Munich, was an international development. Picabia, born in Paris of a Cuban father and a French mother, started it off with his famous water-colour *Rubber,* painted in 1909; and its most ardent exponents in the Paris of the years before the 1914 War were the Czech Kupka, and the Russian Rossiné, one of whose paintings in oil hangs in the Musée d'Art Moderne.

Even more international was Expressionism, which was in vogue in Montparnasse after the illusory victory of 1918. At Montparnasse, on the terraces of the Coupole, the Dôme and the Rotonde, a crowd of artists jostled – artists of every colour, race and nationality, – or in some cases without nationality, a sign of the times. Such was Pascin, born in Bulgaria, his father a Spanish Jew, brought up in Vienna and Munich, living in Paris, leaving it in 1914 for the United States, where he acquired citizenship, finally returning to Paris in 1920 and taking his life there ten years later. Expressionism was international not only in its sources – Toulouse-Lautrec, Rouault and the Picasso of the Blue, Pink, and Negro periods, Munch and the Germans of *Die Brücke* – but equally in its exponents. Among these were the Frenchmen, Le Fauconnier, Gromaire, Goerg, Alix, the young Fautrier; Italy was represented in Montparnasse by Modigliani, Russia by Chagall and Soutine, Poland by Makowski, Mexico by Sarraga, Japan by Foujita. This coming together of artists of diverse native genius (with a special place due to the Jewish race) produced an art which was moving and intense, violent and tormented, but still owing a good deal to France. This debt is at once apparent if one compares its canvases with, for instance, those of Flemish Expressionism, more earthy and more truly indigenous, and which can justly claim a kinship with Brueghel; or again, with those of German Expressionism, more literary, more political, in which the anxiety of the artist to speak his mind and castigate society prevails over the aim of achieving a work that comes off as a painting.

The French tradition contributed to the movement the concern to interpret emotion in spate within the discipline of painting, while at the same time Paris set its own feverish mark on it and imparted a polish and sophistication in sharp contrast with the peasant style of the Belgian Expressionism of the school of Laethem-Saint Martin. If ever the interaction of influences of diverse traditions came to fruition, it was indeed in the art of this 'school of Montparnasse', so resoundingly famous in the 'twenties that it tended to overshadow the other two important movements in painting thriving at the same time and also essentially international.

Certainly no efforts were spared to bring one of these two movements, Surrealism, to the public attention. It was the heir of the strange pictures painted in Paris by Chirico, half-mountebank, half-medium, during 1912–1914; it derived too from the anti-art paraded even before the First World War by Marcel Duchamp and then by

Picabia. An offshoot of the Dada movement which brought together in a neutral Switzerland at the height of the war artists of various nationalities, the Surrealism of Paris drew its recruits mainly from the French, the Germans and the Spaniards – the Catalans rather. From this medley of followers was born the painting which is sometimes anti-art, and which combines in a paradoxical synthesis literature and poetry, inspiration and concoction, both disdain of plastic art and pleasure in it, order and anarchy, the negation of authenticity and real magic at the same time.

The Surrealism of the Frenchmen Masson and Tanguy, the German Max Ernst and the Catalans Miró and Dali (to mention only a few of the chief exponents) was indeed international, – but abstract painting was even more so. However, it led so quiet, modest and withdrawn an existence in Paris from 1919 to 1939 that it was almost unknown to the 'Tout-Paris' of the fashionable world, to the critics and the Press; and even today, when we think of abstract painting, it is not so much Paris that comes to mind as Moscow, Weimar, Dessau, Hanover or the Netherlands. But abstract art was not to flourish for long in Soviet Russia. It was ostracised in 1920, an example that Hitler's Germany was to follow in 1933. In the Netherlands the tradition of freedom meant that no action was taken (quite the contrary) against the exponents of Neo-Plasticism, and yet the artists themselves preferred life in Paris, with all its rigours, to the peaceful charms of Amsterdam, Rotterdam or The Hague: Paris, that Mondrian was in such a hurry to reach again when the end of the First World War made it possible; Paris, from which abstract painting was to set forth to win over the other countries that were still unaware of it – England, the United States and Uruguay especially; Paris, indeed, which attracted from time to time such painters as Gleizes, Fernand Léger and Jacques Villon, and drew in – permanently or for a spell – artists like Herbin and the Delaunays. Thus, quietly, in a kind of half-light, yet another movement began to take shape in which talents of various nationalities blended together to produce a kind of κοινή – a community – in which their respective accents could still be detected.

14

The story of abstract art in Paris is interesting from another point of view: it shows why France alone, in the first decades of the twentieth century, remained the centre of a living art, rather than the other countries which might have been serious rivals – especially Germany and Russia. In 1914 French painting, or that evolved in Paris by Frenchmen or foreigners, was unmatched in its brilliance; Germany too was experiencing a time of intense activity in painting, mainly in Munich where, just as in Paris, a great number of foreigners were at work – especially Russians, such as Kandinsky and Jawlensky. And in Russia itself, awakening for the first time to the idea of pure art, new trends were evident. In Moscow – a city of greater vitality in this respect than Petrograd – art movements broke entirely new ground and were led by artists of astonishing enterprise. There was a moment when artists thought these movements would have success: this was when the Revolution summoned them to take up the direction of the arts in the Soviet Union. Approval and tolerance, alas, were short-lived; Lenin was no sooner dead than Soviet policy in the arts changed, and one after another, the leaders of the Russian *avant-garde* either withdrew into silence and solitude or else took the path of the exile. For some of them – Chagall, Larionov, Gontcharova, Pevsner – this led to Paris. Others, Kandinsky in particular, made their way to Germany, bringing with them vital influences affecting the artistic life that the defeat of 1918, far from depressing, had stimulated. Munich was no longer, as in the time of the Empire, the capital of the arts. This title passed to Weimar and then to Dessau – the home of the *Bauhaus,* undoubtedly the supreme focus of German art between 1920 and 1930.

Berlin was also seeing great activity in painting, but this was halted with the coming of the Nazis. The representatives of 'degenerate art' were hunted down, and took refuge in remote villages where they worked simply for their personal satisfaction, unable to exhibit unless they chose, like Klee, Kandinsky, Feininger, Beckmann and many others, to seek in free countries the liberty to paint as they chose. For Kandinsky, the country was France, which benefited by the errors of artistic judgment of both Russia and Nazi Germany.

However, events were later to take the opposite course. During the Second World War, when Paris and two thirds of France were German-occupied, artists left in their numbers, following the lead of Mondrian, for one, who departed at the outbreak of hostilities. Both foreigners and Frenchmen crossed the Atlantic to seek in the United States, and especially in New York, a more secure place to work. Léger, Masson, Tanguy, Chagall and many others settled there, and their presence and teaching, together with lessons in the art of the Far East, quickly produced a brilliant harvest. It seemed that France would follow Russia and Germany in artistic decline, and that the School of Paris would give place to a School of New York.

This is not in fact what happened. No sooner was France liberated than a fair number of artists re-crossed the Atlantic, as if they must breathe the air between Montparnasse and Montmartre. It is hardly surprising that Frenchmen such as Léger and Masson did so. One is more surprised and flattered that foreign-born artists should return to Paris, which had seen them at work for so many years and where some of them had acquired French nationality. Chagall came back from New York, Vieira da Silva from Rio de Janeiro, other artists from Switzerland where they had found a less distant refuge. Besides the old residents, still faithful to their first love, there was a throng of newcomers who could just as well have remained in their own countries as betaken themselves elsewhere. That they made for Paris seems so strange as to call for an explanation.

Self-portrait, c. 1889, by Edouard Vuillard (1868–1940). Signed. ▷
Oil on canvas: 24 cm.×18 cm.
Presented by M. Hessel, 1942.

This self-portrait, painted by Vuillard in a traditional style before he joined the Nabi group, not only preserves a likeness of the artist at about nineteen years of age, but already reveals his subtle sense of light, colour and execution, as well as the acute perception of the Intimist painter.

16

Why were so many artists from all the countries of Europe, and as far afield as India, China, Korea, Japan, and the Americas, determined to reach Paris and make their home there, despite material difficulties and moral problems? It is not enough to cite the long prestige of the city which had seen Van Gogh at work and where Picasso was still active, and to recall that a hearth where the fire has been extinguished continues to give off a glow for a long time – as with Rome of the second half of the seventeenth and the eighteenth century. In an era when history marches so swiftly and when nothing makes an enduring impression on over-realistic humanity (the tone of which has spread even to the artists), a bygone splendour would be powerless to gather crowds of foreigners to Paris. Nor can it be explained by the first-rate organisation of the fine-arts market of Paris and its expert 'launchings' to reach an international public. Unlike a number of other countries, the French State does nothing at all to promote this trade, and even falls behind on a purely cultural and disinterested plane in 'setting a market value' on its artists.

The sole reason for the phenomenon, then, is the spirit of this ancient city and the atmosphere there, which is especially conducive to the flowering of talents in freedom and independence. Perhaps one might go so far as to say that this atmosphere is even better now than it was during the years, so melancholy in every respect, between the two wars. Painting was marking time then, and despite developments such as Surrealism – more literary in any case than pictorial – the tendency was towards reaction. There was talk only of 'returns' – return to nature, to human values, to tradition. For art to make a new beginning it took nothing less than the occupation of France by a nation dead set against 'decadent art'. If the art of France was to survive and remain French, it followed that it had to take up again the path of the 'dropped' *avant-garde*. French painting pushed off to that fresh start in 1941 with an exhibition with the challenging title 'Exhibition of Young Painters in the French Tradition' – proof enough of the decisive stimulus given by the defeat of 1940 and the Occupation.

Thus, a new generation entered the lists determined to push forward. Its aspirations were so in harmony with the hopes and ambitions of France that it took but two years to win its public. On the heels of Matisse, Picasso, Léger, the Delaunays and their like, came painters worthy of them, such as Bazaine, Estève, Pignon, Manessier. Once it had begun, nothing could halt the triumphant progress of French art, which had regained the bold spirit natural to it. The Salon de Mai was founded in 1945 and the Réalités Nouvelles in 1946; fine painters long unrecognised, such as Bissière, Schneider, Hartung, were given full honour, and there was a break-through to notice by young artists such as Soulages, de Staël and Atlan. These facts and names (among many others) prove that since 1941, French painting had found its vocation again – to forge ahead, to be a powerful astringent, to shatter apathy and complacency, to submit everything to question, to be the best kind of intellectual guide – not providing formulas but pointing the way to self-knowledge through self-examination. It was, in fine, to have a Socratic character.

Paris, the Socratic city! This, in the final count, is the reason for its prestige, based on its artistic fertility. No one will deny the challenge of other cities – New York with its vast economic and political power in particular – to Paris for this sovereign place in the art of our time, once enjoyed by Munich and by Moscow. However, notwithstanding all the trials endured by France since 1940, Paris still remains the most powerful magnet for foreign artists today. The proof of this is the actual presence of these artists from abroad, more active and numerous than ever before, even counting the glorious days of Montparnasse in the 'twenties. Now as then, the French and the foreigners interact upon each other, providing the present School of Paris with its strongest and most effective cement: collaboration in a common task. French native genius encounters that of these other countries to the great benefit of contemporary art and of civilization as a whole. For instance, there comes to mind the art of Zao-Wou-Ki, where the pure strain of Far Eastern tradition comes alive and draws strength from its contact with Western art; conversely, in the painting of, say, Soulages, the most ancient tradition of the West – the

Romanesque – is seen enriched by the element of Far Eastern calligraphy. An art that is in the full sense humanist, attuned to this world of ours, has thus been evolved in Paris rather than in another city, because it is here more than elsewhere, in this exhilarating Babel, that the native genius of each country meets and challenges that of the others, under the benign eye of French culture which, as ever, stands for tolerance and freedom.

Many countries and cities, of course, have produced painters who are rooted in their native place and owe little or nothing to French painting and the School of Paris. To mention only a few, the most representative, there are the Belgians, Ensor and Permeke; the Austrian Kokoschka; the Spaniard Solana; the Mexicans, Orozco and Tamayo. Still, despite such notable exceptions, it is not unreasonable to claim that the attraction of Paris remains supreme with artists the world over.

Paris and France, therefore, have an obligation to offer these artists, who often enough have only seen reproductions, an adequate survey of the work of the School of Paris, and of the successive art movements since 1890. This duty the Musée d'Art Moderne has tried to fulfill, and in the pages that follow will be found the history, and an analysis, of some of the most renowned of its pictures.

ORIGIN OF THE MUSÉE NATIONAL D'ART MODERNE

Among the twenty-five or so French National Museums of Art, the Musée d'Art Moderne has a rather special place, and for three reasons. First, whilst the other museums keep their collections permanently, the Musée d'Art Moderne possesses them only temporarily. According to the rules, the works are assigned to it for keeping only until the hundredth anniversary of the artist's birth. After that date they leave the gallery, either for the Louvre, or to add to the collection of some museum in the provinces, or to sleep forgotten in some reserve or other set aside for them.

The second peculiarity of the Musée d'Art Moderne is the method of acquisition. In the case of works by artists who have since died, or of works given or bequeathed (whether or not the artist is still living) the procedure is like that of all the other French national museums – purchases are decided by the Comité des Conservateurs des Musées Nationaux and the Conseil des Musées, and are financed by the Réunion des Musées Nationaux. The purchase of works of a living artist, on the other hand, comes within the province of the Direction-Générale des Arts et des Lettres, which each year allocates some of its acquisitions to the Musée d'Art Moderne, the remainder being assigned either to provincial museums or to Ministries, the Prefectures (of *départements*), the Town Halls, Embassies and so on – in short, to any of the countless departments and branches of the French Government. The wisdom of the selection during 1960 can be judged from the exhibition of the cream of the works in the Musée d'Art Moderne in March and April 1961. Besides a collection of twelve ceramics by Picasso, three drawings by Jacques Villon and works by Gromaire and Arp, there were more than a hundred exhibits – paintings, sculpture, water-colours and drawings, signed by some of the best artists of the rising generation. Among the painters and sculptors represented, French or naturalized, were Adam, Bazaine, Beaudin,

César, Cortot, Coutaud, Olivier Debré, Despierre, Dmitrienko, Dubuffet, Estève, Masson, Pignon, Singier, Soulages, Szenes, Tal Coat, Vieira da Silva, and Léon Zack. Foreign artists had not been overlooked, whether they belonged to the School of Paris or not; among them were the Belgians, Alechinsky and Ubac, the Swiss Giacometti and Muller, the Italians Campigli, Music and Severini, the Russians Larionov and Poliakoff, the Pole Lebenstein, the Israeli Achiam, the Mexican Tamayo, as well as the Chinese Zao-Wou-Ki and the Japanese Imai, Sato and Tabuchi. A good number of these works will be allocated to the Musée d'Art Moderne to swell its collection of young artists, that is to say – for art is a great preserver of youth – artists who are not yet fifty to fifty-five years old.

Added to the museum's special arrangements for acquiring its treasures and its service as a transit museum or clearing-house for works of art, with a continuous renewal of its exhibits, the Musée has a third unusual feature: it is at once the most recent and one of the oldest art museums in France. It was in fact opened on 9th June 1947 by Pierre Bourdan, Minister for 'La Jeunesse, des Arts et des Lettres'. On the other hand, it was the heir of the old Musée du Luxembourg, founded by Louis XVIII and opened to the public on 11th April 1818.

Moreover, the royal Musée du Luxembourg, intended for the works of living artists (as laid down by Royal Decree) had a history almost a century long. The Superintendent of Fine Arts, Lenormand de Tournehem, had decided in 1750 to assemble in a gallery of the Luxembourg some canvases belonging to the royal collections and to admit the public. The criticisms of this arrangement, and the establishment in 1778 of the Comte de Provence in the Palais du Luxembourg, led Marigny to transfer these works to the Louvre. Then came the Revolution. The Luxembourg was turned first into a prison, then into the town house of a member of the Directory and finally, under the Consulate, it became the seat of the Conservative Senate. In 1808 Chaptal, Minister of the Interior, took the opportunity to hang series of paintings in the east wing: Rubens' *Life of Marie de Medici*, Le Sueur's *Life of St Bruno* and Joseph Vernet's *Ports of France*.

The paintings were not to remain there for long. In 1815 they were transferred to the Louvre to take the place of the works which had been pillaged in foreign countries by the Revolutionary and Imperial armies, and which Napoleon in his defeat had been obliged to restore to their owners. It was then that, in order to refill the Musée du Luxembourg, Louis XVIII had the idea, surprisingly original for the period, of turning it into a gallery reserved for living painters. This was certainly the first time that a museum had been assigned to art that was still in the process of development. David, Prud'hon, Guérin and Girodet were thus given the first honours of this museum, known at the time as the Musée de Chambre des Pairs.

As the preserve of the neo-classicism of David, it opened its doors unwillingly to Ingres, and even less willingly to the young Géricault and Delacroix of the Romantic movement. But the day came when the Second Republic and then the Second Empire made an effort to throw the doors wider open to those known as the '1830 painters', such as Corot, Théodore Rousseau, Jules Dupré and Troyon, and even to the '1848 painters', like Millet and Courbet.

The Third Republic followed a less liberal policy than the two earlier régimes, and the Musée du Luxembourg became the almost exclusive show-place of the academic triumphs of the Salon and the Institut de France. Bonnat, Bouguereau, Detaille and Gérôme carried the honours there, while the Government, the authorities and public opinion clamoured – happily in vain – in favour of refusing the Caillebotte Bequest. This boasted four Manets, seven Degas, sixteen Monets, eighteen Pissarros, nine Sisleys, eight Renoirs, five Cézannes, and others – a total of sixty-seven paintings, of which thirty-eight only were finally accepted.

The Museum had meanwhile moved house. From 1876 to 1886 it had occupied a rough wooden structure built on the terrace between the two pavilions that give on to the rue de Vaugirard, but it was turned out by the Senate, which objected to this hospitality. They did, however, end by granting the Museum a home in the Orangery of the Palace, and it was in the Orangery, enlarged by a small pavilion built to house the Caillebotte Bequest, that the Museum carried on its life from 1886 to 1939. Soon it became far too crowded, and in order to relieve the congestion the foreign works were removed, – even those by foreign painters settled in Paris, unless they had been naturalised. These works formed a new art gallery, the Jeu de Paume. The Caillebotte Collection was transferred to the Louvre, with some other Impressionist pictures from the old Luxembourg. Then it was noticed that the Orangery held hardly anything of value. Louis Hautecœur, today permanent secretary of the Académie des Beaux-Arts, first set about remedying the situation, aided by his deputy curator, Pierre Ladoué.

To get some idea of the narrow scope of the collections in the Musée du Luxembourg at the time, it is only necessary to look through the 1930 Catalogue, almost contemporary with the above appointments. The Nabis are represented by four Bonnards, of no great importance, four works of Maurice Denis, four of Vuillard, including the splendid *Gardens of Paris,* bought in 1929 at the Natanson sale. Fauvism is still poorly represented. Marquet is indeed there with six paintings (all later than his Fauve period), but Matisse has only two works, one being the *Buffet* presented in 1929 by the Association des Amis des Artistes Vivants. Certainly there are two Van Dongens of which one was given by the same society, and also two Vlamincks, two of Friesz, and three Derains – of which *Forest* and *Woman's Head* were gifts of the Société des Amis du Luxembourg. Dufy and Rouault, on the other hand, are unrepresented. Cubism is even more neglected. There was no work by Braque, Delaunay, Gleizes, La Fresnaye, Fernand Léger, Metzinger or Jacques Villon. André Lhote alone is tolerated, with four small pictures. There is not a single Neo-primitive or Surrealist, and there are few Expressionists, save La Patellière. As for the painters who are not to be classified under any school, it is true that Sir Joseph Duveen had given two landscapes by Utrillo, but Utrillo's mother Suzanne Valadon, Dufresne and Dunoyer de Segonzac are represented by only a single work apiece. Sculpture fared little better. It is true the Musée possessed at that time seven works by Bourdelle and five by Despiau, but it had only two by Maillol and none at all by Arp, Laurens or Duchamp-Villon. The position at the

Musée du Jeu de Paume was similar: of the foreign painters working in Paris, Picasso was unrepresented until 1933, Juan Gris until 1935, and Marcoussis until 1937. There was no Modigliani until 1932, only one Chagall, no Brancusi, Gargallo, Gonzalèz, Lipchitz or Zadkine. The task which confronted M. Dezarrois, curator of the Jeu de Paume, must have seemed as formidable as that of his colleagues at the Luxembourg.

The problem was squarely met, and in 1940, when Louis Hautecœur left the Luxembourg to become Director of Fine Arts, thanks to him and his two successive deputy-curators, Ladoué and Jean Cassou, five important works by Bonnard had been added to the existing four – the *Peignoir*, the *Maison de Missia*, the *Red bodice*, bought in 1938 at the Fontaine sale, the *Corner of the dining room, Le Cannet*, and the incomparable *Corner of the table*. Paintings by Vuillard were increased in number from five to nine and those by Maurice Denis from four to six. Similar progress was made with the Fauves: the *Decorative figure on an ornamental background* of Matisse was acquired in 1938, as well as seven Marquets (including the masterly *Portrait of André Rouveyre)*, five Vlamincks, four Friesz, six Derains and one Van Dongen; Dufy and Rouault were represented at last, the first by a *The Paddock at Deauville* and a set of drawings, the second by a *The Holy Face* presented in 1933 by Mrs Chester Dale and a landscape of 1907 bought in 1938.

Maurice Utrillo, his grandmother and his dog, 1910, ▷
by Suzanne Valadon (1867–1938). Signed. Oil on cardboard: 70 cm.×50 cm. Purchased by the State.

The '*grande Suzanne*', as her admirers call her, has here brought together two models who were especially dear to her, her old mother, '*Maman Madeleine*' and her son, then twenty-seven years old. The Musée d'Art Moderne owns another portrait of Utrillo by his mother, a drawing done when he was about five or six years old.

Braque also passed the doors hitherto closed to the Cubists, and three of his canvases were acquired, including the *Duet* of 1937. La Fresnaye was now represented by nine paintings, gouaches and drawings, among them one of his chief works, the *Cuirassier* of 1910, acquired in 1938. Another fine painting, the *Wedding* by Fernand Léger (1911) was presented in 1937 by Alfred Flechtheim. Space was found for Delaunay with two oils, for Gleizes with two gouaches and for Jacques Villon with a single canvas. The collection of works by André Lhote had been increased by three. Expressionism was no longer ostracised; some idea of it was given by one La Patellière, two Goergs and four Gromaires. Even Surrealism was admitted, with a canvas by Tanguy. There were also seven Dufresnes, two canvases by Dunoyer de Segonzac, one Utrillo, and three new Suzanne Valadons. There was a like improvement where sculpture was concerned, with a wise selection of Bourdelle, Despiau, Pompon and Maillol. In the space of nine years, the curators had brought living art to the former bastion of academic tradition.

However, another problem arose: the Orangery of the Senate, which had been able to house the Musée very adequately since 1886, was rapidly becoming short of space. Consideration had to be given to housing the growing collections in a more spacious building. The International Exhibition of 1937 came opportunely to allow the building of a larger art gallery. The site found was that of the former *Manutention,* which had to be shared with the City of Paris, also anxious to have a gallery of modern art. It was on sloping ground, enclosed between the Seine and the high ground of Chaillot, badly served by transport and in a quarter which was becoming less residential yet was not entirely commercial. The new site was far from having the value of the old one of the Musée du Luxembourg, but at least it was appreciably larger. A competition was held for the design of the museum, in which prominent architects, such as Perret and Le Corbusier, took part. The selection committee, presided over by M. Pontremoli, chose the plans of three young architects, Aubert, Dondel and Viard, who had only recently qualified at the Ecole des Beaux-Arts; they were joined by a colleague of greater renown,

Dastugue. The building, unlike most of those for the 1937 Exhibition, was ready for the opening and served as a setting for one of the most prodigious assemblies of art treasures ever seen, the impressive exhibition of *Chefs d'œuvre de l'Art Français*. Those who saw it are unlikely ever to forget it. But this exhibition had demonstrated the serious drawbacks of the building itself. As soon as its doors had been closed a remedy had to be found and the curators pointed out various changes that were imperative. This work delayed the transfer of the collections from the Musée du Luxembourg to the new building, called by the public the Palais de Tokyo because it was on the avenue of that name. When all was ready for the move in 1939, the Second World War broke out.

The main works were sent to the store-houses in the Loire Valley, while the remainder were transferred to the reserves of the Musée d'Art Moderne and would no doubt have remained there until the end of the War had not the declared intention of the Germans in 1942 to requisition this empty building led Louis Hautecœur and his colleagues to decide on a partial opening. The best items were brought up from the reserves, and some of the most notable paintings were returned from the store-houses, including the *Odalisque in red pantaloons* of Matisse, the *Holy Face* by Rouault, the *Duet* by Braque, and the *Cuirassier* by La Fresnaye. A provisional opening took place in August, 1942.

Although slowed down by the Occupation, the process of making acquisitions to the Musée went on. For example, Dunoyer de Segonzac's *Landscape, St Tropez*, and La Patellière's masterly *Rest in the cellar*, were purchased. And the gallery came into possession of the Barthellemy donation, the Paul Jamot bequest and the Vuillard donation. The first of these included such contemporary masterpieces as Bonnard's *Beach at Arcachon*, Utrillo's *Lapin Agile*, La Fresnaye's *Poet* and the *Sea at Le Havre* by Dufy. The Jamot collection, built up with the unerring taste of the distinguished former Conservateur-en-Chef of the Department of Paintings at the Louvre, included canvases by Bonnard, Maurice Denis, Dufy, Dunoyer de Segonzac, Marquet and others. The third gift, that of Vuillard, brought the

Musée fifty-four of the painter's own works, and of them it retained for its own walls some of the finest in the present collection – the astonishing *Au Lit,* for instance, the *Red dining-room, Walk by the harbour, Cargo-boat alongside the quay,* and others.

The Musée, half-open as it was in August 1942, was not to remain so for long. Fifteen months later the chief paintings were again sent to the store-houses and the others were put in the reserves of the Musée, which was closed until the end of the Occupation. It was re-opened to a limited extent and at intervals in October 1944 and in May and October 1945, to house the exhibitions devoted to the Douanier Rousseau, Maurice Denis, and La Patellière, before making room in the spring and summer of 1946 for the unrivalled exhibition of French tapestries. By the time this exhibition came to an end, having been seen by more than a hundred thousand visitors, it had created such a stir that Pierre Verlet had to take it on to Brussels, Amsterdam, London, New York, Chicago, Montreal, and elsewhere.

Plans had now to be made for the permanent opening of the Musée, to which had been added the former Musée des Ecoles Etrangères Contemporaines, housed since 1930 in the Jeu de Paume of the Tuileries. And indeed how absurd it would have been to exhibit at the Musée d'Art Moderne the work of foreigners such as Van Dongen, Chagall and Zadkine on the score of their naturalization, while excluding the works of Picasso, Gris or Miró, who had kept their Spanish nationality. The move to the Jeu de Paume of the Musée de l'Impressionisme put an end to this confusion. The Musée d'Art Moderne took in the collections of the former Musée du Jeu de Paume, works by both the painters of the School of Paris and those who had stayed in their own countries.

In making an inventory of the outstanding works in the Musée d'Art Moderne, however, it was seen that despite all efforts since 1931, the finest contemporary painters were still inadequately represented. Energetic endeavours were necessary if they were to figure appropriately in time for the opening. This was seen clearly by Jacques Jaujard, Directeur-général des Arts et des Lettres, and Georges Salles, Directeur des Musées, whose discriminating taste and enthusiasm for contemporary art were decisive assets, and by David Weill, chairman of the Conseil des Musées, who persuaded Jean Cassou to make the necessary purchases during the winter of 1946–1947. M. Cassou had the advantage of long-standing friendship with the best-known painters of the day; he enjoyed public renown for his heroism during the Occupation and at the time of the Liberation, was well-known as a man of letters, and had had long years of experience at the Luxembourg. The Museum owes to him the acquisition of four masterpieces by Bonnard (including *Woman dozing on a bed* and *In the boat)*; three dazzling canvases by Vlaminck; seven Matisses (including *Le Luxe*, *Painter and his model* and *Red still-life with magnolia*); five Braques (among them the *Salon* and the *Billiard-table*), five Rouaults, two Gris, one Dufy, and others. Picasso generously added to his sole canvas from the Jeu de Paume (the *Portrait of Gustave Coquiot)* a set of ten paintings, among which were the famous *Dressmaker's Work-room* and *Aubade*. Other donations arrived in the nick of time, such as the Lurçat tapestry, *The Storm,* presented by Georges Salles, as well as an important work by Braque, one Picasso, two fine Maria Blanchards, one remarkable Lhote, four outstanding canvases by Léger, a charming work by Marie Laurencin and three canvases by Masson – all among the items given by M. Paul Rosenberg. The gallery opened its doors to the public on 9th June 1947, and as Georges Salles rightly remarked, this day 'ended the divorce between State and genius.'

THE DEVELOPMENT OF THE MUSÉE

Since the museum's opening day in 1947 its staff have not slackened in their efforts; as many as ninety exhibitions have been held, some of which have created world-wide interest. In 1952, for example, there was the exhibition of Mexican Art, in 1958 the Japanese Art exhibition, and more recently, the memorable exhibition of the 'Sources of Twentieth Century Art' organized by Jean Cassou under the auspices of the Council of Europe. In addition to these major exhibitions, there have been many smaller ones which have brought to Paris the works of contemporary foreign artists, hitherto little known in France, or have illustrated the contribution to art of a French movement or of a great French painter towards the end of his career or posthumously. For example, there have been special exhibitions of the work of Ensor, Permeke, Kutter, Henry Moore, Wotruba, Klee, Kandinsky, Torres Garcia, Alfred Pellan; of Dutch painting since Van Gogh, Swiss painting from Hodler to Klee, contemporary Italian art, the work of a dozen modern Polish painters, Norwegian mural painting, Russian art from Peter the Great to the present day, fifty years of art in the United States, the primitives of Haiti, and so on. Among the most remarkable exhibitions in the second category have been those of the art of the Nabis (1955), of Fauvism (1951), of Cubism (1953), and those in honour of Suzanne Valadon, Signac, Matisse, Marquet, Dufy, Henri Laurens, Rouault, Derain, La Fresnaye, Jacques Villon, Léger, Robert Delaunay, Zadkine, Lipchitz, Gonzalèz, Pevsner, Le Corbusier, Bissière, Walch, Gruber, Nicolas de Staël and Germaine Richier. Not only have these artists become better known and appreciated through these special exhibitions, but the public which has been drawn to the new Musée by them has returned to enjoy the permanent collections.

These permanent collections have been added to considerably between June 1947 and April 1961, both by gifts and by means of purchases by the Direction-Générale des Arts et des Lettres. The number of paintings in the possession of the Musée has risen during these fourteen years from 2,744 to 3,920, the number of sculptures from 852 to 1,160, and of drawings, water-colours, gouaches and pastels from 1,722 to 2,235.

One result of this vast increase was that the small collection of engravings built up since 1935 had to be housed elsewhere. This has gone, appropriately, to the Cabinet des Estampes in the Bibliothèque Nationale, where there is special provision for the care of engravings. The few pieces of furniture that had been in the possession of the Musée d'Art Moderne since 1937, and most of the applied art exhibits, were transferred to the Garde-meuble (State repositories). The Musée retained only a few tapestries, evidence of the magnificent revival of this craft in France since 1939, together with some ceramics, specimens of stained glass and enamels by such famous artists as Rouault, Dufy, Braque, Picasso, Léger, Miró. These exceptions apart, shortage of space and staff has obliged the Musée d'Art Moderne to confine itself to painting, sculpture and drawings, and especially to the works of the School of Paris since the 1890's. Even so, to make room for all its exhibits, the layout of the Musée had to be redesigned. The long halls stretching from one end of the Musée to the other were divided into small rooms. On the suggestion of Le Corbusier, some of the partitions were painted in bright colours – vermilion, canary yellow, prussian blue, orange – chosen naturally to suit the pictures to be hung on them. Other walls were velvet-covered; on others again, an interesting experiment was tried with the use of an incombustible fibre-glass background.

With these readjustments, the Musée has provided hanging space for an ever-increasing number of works. By 1961 the number of Bonnards had reached twenty-eight and the Vuillards thirty-seven. The collection of Rouaults has been increased since 1947 by seven paintings and the *Miserere* etchings. Ten paintings by Matisse have been added, as well as one *papier collé*, two sculptures and half-a-dozen drawings. Dufy was poorly represented at first, but now he is exhibited in a truly splendid manner with six more paintings, three ceramics and two drawings, as well as the definitive version of his *Fée Electricité*. The number of Marquets has reached nineteen, and two Derains, three Friesz, one Camoin and one Van Dongen, all of their Fauve period, now represent one of the greatest moments in French contemporary art. Among the Cubist works, the Braques have reached sixteen, with one sculpture, and the Picassos now number twenty-two paintings, with one *papier collé*, two drawings, one terra-cotta and thirteen ceramics. Léger is represented by twenty-seven works, La Fresnaye by twenty-four, Villon by eighteen, Gleizes by eight, and Delaunay by ten – comprising oil paintings, gouaches, water-colours, pastels, drawings, *papiers collés*, and so on. Although it was 1954 before the first Marcel Duchamp was exhibited *(Chess players)*, the Parisian origins of Abstract painting are recalled by Delaunay's *Circular Forms*, by the canvases of his wife, Sonia Terk-Delaunay, by a painting of Rossiné dated February 1910, a collection of about twenty Kupkas, and also by two especially precious pictures – Picabia's *Rubber* (1909), and his *Udnie*, painted four years later with astonishing verve and mastery.

A particular pride of the Musée are the thirteen Chagalls, the eleven Bissières, the Le Corbusiers, the Duchamp-Villons, the Brancusis; and the splendid collection of 'twentieth-century primitives', consisting of works by Séraphine, Vivin, Bombois, Bauchant, Peyronnet, Jean Eve, Rimbert, Caillard, Desnos and others. The doors of the Musée were now open to *avant-garde* painting. Gifts and purchases have brought in a whole range, from figurative artists such as Pignon and André Marchand to non-figurative painters like Bazaine, Manessier, Singier and Le Moal; from orthodox abstract painters such as Soulages, Hartung, Schneider, Atlan, Mathieu, to those who may or may not be abstract, such as Vieira da Silva, Estève, Zao-Wou-Ki, Busse, Cortot, Dmitrienko and Nicolas de Staël.

The gifts and bequests to the Musée played a larger part in the growth of collections even than purchases. Although the Musée has received no single large bequests, such as that of the Caillebotte collection or the Camondo and Moreau-Nélaton bequests to the Louvre, it has had a great number of gifts making a truly dazzling array. Some donors have qualified their generosity by a justifiable clause of usufruct or life interest. In other cases such clauses have been withdrawn: M. and Mme André Lefèvre, for instance, have made over to the Musée masterpieces by Picasso, La Fresnaye, Modigliani, Léger *(Réveil matin* and *Contrast in forms)*, and Beaudin's *Les Oiseaux blancs*. In 1947 the poet Paul Eluard gave the portrait of his wife by Picasso, and Mme Jenny Bernard made over to the Musée her portrait by Van Dongen. Another of his portraits, that of Mme Jasmy Alvin, was bequeathed in the same year by the sitter for the picture. The year 1948 was especially fruitful. The generosity of Mlle Uhde, M. Franz Meyer and an anonymous lady donor made it possible to arrange a special room for the 'twentieth-century primitives', inscribed with the name of the connoisseur Wilhelm Uhde. In the same year the collections of Vuillard and La Fresnaye were augmented by the Xavier Fontaine bequest and Germain Seligmann donation. Also, Jean Aron stripped his own walls to make over a collection of canvases to the Musée, among them Van Dongen's *Saltimbanque aux seins nus* and La Fresnaye's *Nudes in a landscape*. Mme Abreu gave a Vuillard, a Luc-Albert Moreau and two Boussingaults.

In 1949, Philippe Fontaine presented Vuillard's portrait of his father, the patron of the arts Arthur Fontaine, and in 1951, Mme Huc de Montfreid gave a dozen works belonging to her father, a

Matisse painting from a model in Manguin's studio, 1905,　　　▷
by Albert Marquet (1875–1947). Signed. Oil on canvas: 100 cm.×73 cm.
Presented by M. Pierre David-Weill, 1957.

Matisse and Marquet, great friends as they were, had a close association too with the painter Manguin, and it was in his studio at 61, rue Boursault that each painted the other while they were both working from the same model, a female nude. The Musée is fortunate in possessing both portraits. Manguin, too, painted a canvas from this model, which is now in the Stein Collection, U.S.A.

friend of Gauguin's. It was in that same year that the Vicomte de Noailles gave a Giacometti and M. and Mme Gaston Bernheim de Villers two Vuillard portraits, two by Vallotton and a Bonnard masterpiece, the *Portrait of the brothers Bernheim*. Two major works of Picasso came to the Musée in 1952, with a Gris, *Still-life on a chair*, Braque's *Side table* (1911) and *Black side table* (1922), all presented by Raoul La Roche of Basle, who added Braque's *Woman with a guitar* in 1957 and the *Relief in painted wire* by his fellow-countryman, Bodmer, in 1960.

Two considerable bequests came in 1953. One was from Mme Natanson, widow of the well-known Thadée Natanson, founder of the *Revue Blanche* and first patron of the Nabis; the other was from Carle Dreyfus, former Conservateur en Chef of the Département des Objets d'Art in the Louvre. The Natanson bequest included important works by Maillol, Vuillard's *Woman darning* and *Portrait of Thadée Natanson*, and a Bonnard, *Portrait of Marthe Bonnard and Reine Natanson*. From the Dreyfus bequest there came fine paintings by Vuillard and Vallotton, and a magnificent portfolio of drawings by artists such as Bonnard, Marquet and Segonzac. The year 1954, too, was marked by a notable bequest, that of Maurice Meunier, which brought to the Musée two Picassos (a *Woman's torso* of Alexandrian grace and *Nature morte à la charlotte*), a Miró, a Chirico, and a Marcoussis worthy of Braque, the *Bowl of gold-fish*, of 1925. In 1957, Pierre David-Weill made over two superb portraits, Marquet's *Matisse painting from a model*, and Matisse's painting of Marquet working on the identical subject. With the second came a sketch of astonishing verve, a preparation for the canvas Matisse painted in 1905 in the studio of Manguin.

Two years later, in 1959, the Comtesse Blanche de Polignac left to the Musée two portraits by Vuillard, her own and that of her mother Jeanne Lanvin. In the same year M. and Mme Jacques Dubourg presented a fine painting by Nicolas de Staël, *Le Lavandou*. The following year, two drawings by Léger came to fill a gap in our collection; these were presented by Kahnweiler, who had already made a handsome gift to the Musée in 1957, a terra-cotta *Head* by

Picasso. Other art dealers were equally generous: Pierre Loeb gave a *Landscape* by Miró; Larcade, a vast canvas by Mathieu, *Les Capétiens partout*; Georges Wildenstein made over two canvases by Masson; and an especially moving gift came from Clayeux, who brought *Wind off the Sea* by Bazaine in memory of Bernard Maeght.

Early in 1961 the Musée had a great stroke of good fortune; it received fifty-eight works as a bequest of M. and Mme Lung of Algiers. These included Bonnard's *Dressing-table*, a miracle of grace and light, an *Interior* by Matisse, three Marquets painted in North Africa, a *Still-life with tea pot* by La Fresnaye, truly Greek in its flow of line, three water-colours by Segonzac and a collection of a dozen works by Dufresne.

In a review of all these contributions one is particularly struck by the generosity shown by artists and their relatives. There is hardly a distinguished artist, young or old, who has not shown appreciation of the Musée in some practical way—a splendid example is that of Picasso in 1947. Matisse gave the *Roumanian Blouse*, six of his finest drawings, a printed textile designed by him, and a landscape by his old friend, Jean Puy. Mme Raoul Dufy presented two important works by her husband, the *Three bathers* and *Riders under the trees*. Mme Marquet, too, gave two canvases and sixteen masterly drawings by her husband, as well as the portrait of him by Camoin. Mme Friesz even presented her own portrait by Friesz, as well as a drawing by him. Rouault has enriched the Musée's collections by the well-known *Homo homini lupus*. Braque, for his part, gave his splendid *Black fish* and his sculpture, *Horse's head*. Léger made over his *Composition with parrots*, his *Adieu, New York* and one of his tapestries. Jacques Villon gave his moving portrait of his brother, the sculptor Raymond Duchamp-Villon, and Mme Delaunay the *Manège de cochons* by Robert Delaunay, two canvases by herself, a canvas by Gondouin, one by Russolo and one by Jacouvloff. Gleizes contributed his superb *Portrait of Florent Schmitt*; Mme Kupka the *Disks* by her husband; Max Ernst, one of his best canvases, *Après moi, le sommeil*, and Miró his fine *Bull-fight*. Two paintings by La Patellière, one by Segonzac, four by Foujita, a dozen by Pougny, were given by the respective artists or by their widows. Desnoyer used the proceeds of the Prix Opera that he was awarded in 1949 to purchase, on the suggestion of the Musée d'Art Moderne, a large composition by his old friend, Charles Walch, who had not long since died at an early age.

Sculptors, young and old, have been equally generous. There have been presentations by Laurens, Zadkine, Pevsner and his wife, and Mme Roberta Gonzalèz. The older sculptors made available to the Musée a remarkable painting by André Marchand, a dozen drawings by Manessier, a dozen drawings by Pignon, four pastels by Hartung, a sculpture by César, a masterly painting by Soulages, and perhaps the masterpiece of the late Nicolas de Staël, his fine *Roofs*.

The generosity of Chagall and his daughter has enabled us to devote a whole room to him. Bissière and Le Corbusier have done the same for their works. Mme Despiau first lent in 1959, and then bequeathed a year later, some two hundred sculptures and two hundred drawings by her husband. Then Brancusi left the contents of his studio to the Musée and the funds to adapt one of the rooms for these works; the result has been to make this the finest and most comprehensive collection in the world of this distinguished sculptor's work.

Besides the artists, their relatives and the collectors, there is another patron to whom the Musée is greatly indebted: the Société des Amis du Musée National d'Art Moderne, to which a subsidiary, the Association des Amis des Artistes Vivants, was for a time affiliated. It was founded in 1903 as the Société des Amis du Luxembourg, and contributed to that Musée works which are today the pride of the Musée de l'Impressionisme, such as the famous *Portrait of Madame Charpentier* by Renoir. Some time later, under the chairmanship of the late Charles Pacquement, the Société was responsible for adding to the Musée's collections, among other works, two Derains, one Dufresne, the *Paddock at Deauville* by Dufy, two works by Dunoyer de Segonzac, one Fautrier, one Gromaire, two paintings by La Fresnaye, one Laprade, two Lhotes, one Lurçat, the *Buffet* by Matisse, and the *Spanish Dancer* and the *Fellahs* by Van Dongen. The

Société des Amis du Musée National d'Art Moderne became very active indeed under Georges Grammont, to whom Saint-Tropez owes its Musée de l'Annonciade – undoubtedly the finest collection of contemporary painting to be seen in France, after the Musée d'Art Moderne, the Musée d'Art Moderne de la Ville de Paris and the Musée de Grenoble. His good work was continued by Maurice Bérard, the tireless organizer of exhibitions to help the funds of the society, and with his flair and enthusiasm the discoverer of unlooked-for bargains. Under these two chairmen, so different in character and temperament, how many masterpieces have found their way into the Musée's collections! In 1951 there was Braque's *Landscape, l'Estaque,* and in 1952 *The painter's studio at Perpignan*, by Dufy; in 1953, the *Still-life with egg-cup* by Roger de la Fresnaye; in 1955, the *Route de Clamart* by Matisse; in 1957, Dufy's definitive version of his stupendous *Fée Electricité*; in 1958, Metzinger's *Landscape* and the *Sacrifice of Iphigenia* by Dufresne; in 1959, Kandinsky's masterpiece *Ambiguity*; in 1960, the *Cène sur la Seine* by the fascinating naive painter Fernand Desnos; and in 1961 a large drawing by Picasso, *Danseuse et Picador*, and one of the most distinguished works of Robert Delaunay, his *Circular Forms* of 1912–1913. The Musée has indeed been fortunate in receiving these numerous gifts and bequests, its chief enrichment during the years 1947 to 1961.

THE FUTURE PLANS OF THE MUSÉE

The Musée d'Art Moderne is indeed proud to possess the following: twenty-nine Bonnards,[1] thirty-seven Vuillards, sixteen Dufys, twenty-six Matisses, twenty-three Marquets, nineteen Rouaults, nineteen Braques, thirty-eight Picassos, twenty-five Légers, thirteen La Fresnayes, thirteen Jacques Villons, ten Delaunays, fourteen Chagalls, in addition to the splendid collections of Maillol, Despiau, Pompon, Duchamp-Villon, Laurens and Brancusi; it is, too, so amply provided as to be able to send numerous works to be exhibited in many museums in the provinces, including a complete collection, the Wakefield-Mori Donation, lent to the Menton Museum. But for all that, the Conservateurs are far from resting on their laurels, and are well aware that a formidable task still remains to be accomplished.

In the first place, the best collections can always be improved. Again, some painters of the School of Paris are still very inadequately represented, for instance Soutine and Modigliani, to name only two. Examples of the work of younger painters must be added to as their art develops. But two needs above all are imperative – the systematic provision of a collection of drawings, which so far has been left to chance good fortune, and the suitable representation of contemporary foreign art, which is virtually non-existent in the Musée.

It is true the Musée is well provided with drawings, water-colours, gouaches and pastels by Vuillard, Matisse, Dufy, Marquet, La Fresnaye, Metzinger, Segonzac, Dufresne, Pignon, Manessier, and Despiau, but the Drawings Room is rather poor in works by other artists is these media. This is the gap which must be filled methodically if those distinguished in the graphic arts, water-colour or gouache are to be given their rightful place.

---

[1] Excluding drawings, but including sculpture, ceramics, tapestries, enamels, etc.

Above all a collection should be built up, necessarily small, but representative, of world art of the twentieth century. Certainly Belgium is represented by Ensor, Jakob Smits, Evenspoel, Van Rysselberghe, Masereel, Wouters and Permeke, but where are Brusselmans, Gustave de Smet, Fritz van den Berghe, Magritte and Delvaux? Examples of Dutch Neo-Plasticism, too, are lacking. Germany's contribution to painting, so important between 1905 and 1933, is represented by Corinth, Rohlfs, Grosz, Beckmann, Baumeister, and, of course, Kandinsky. Klee figures with a mediocre gouache, *Storm passing over a plain*, and an enchanting pastel, *Zauber Blühen*, recently presented by M. Berggruen. Three remarkable canvases by Feininger, Otto Dix and Kirchner have recently been acquired. But nothing in the Musée represents the associates of Kirchner or the art of Marc, Macke or Jawlensky. There is a similar gap in Swiss painting, represented only by a mediocre Hodler, a middling Auberjonois, two delightful water-colours by Moilliet and an abstract work by Bodmer. Among the Italians, who were so productive in the first half of the twentieth century, Balla, Russolo, and Severini alone represent the important Futurist movement, and Chirico, Metaphysical painting. Campigli, Carra, Casorati, de Pisis, Medardo Rosso, Marino Marini are seen only in rather uncharacteristic canvases, and the younger painters are not there at all.

There are no Spaniards except Solana, whose three large compositions so well evoke 'Casticismo'. One Portuguese alone appears, Amadeo de Souza Cardoso, whose delightful canvas was hung in 1959. There are some interesting examples of Spanish-American art in the Musée, especially the works of Figari, Torres Garcia, Portinari, Matta and Tamayo. Art from the United States, so fruitful since 1940, is represented only by a mobile of Calder, while two canvases by Pellan give but an inadequate idea of art in Canada. The revival of interest in sculpture in England is shown in work by Gaudier-Brzeska, Henry Moore, Chadwick and Armitage; canvases by Paul Nash, Sutherland and William Scott represent contemporary *avant-garde* painting there. A fairly adequate collection of Larionov and Gontcharova bears witness to the brief flowering of Russian *avant-garde* painting on the eve of the First World War, but on the other hand, Malevitch and Rodchenko are absent. That great figure in Scandinavian painting, Munch, has no place; Austrian art fares no better for there is no work of Kokoschka. And so it remains one of the most pressing tasks for the Conservateurs of the Musée d'Art Moderne to fill these gaps (and many others too), by acquiring works which will provide typical examples of an artist's genius, and at the same time illustrate art movements of capital importance. Only in this way can the Musée, which now has an excellent collection of French art of this century, give some idea at least of the art of the rest of the world in our time.

MODERN PAINTING AND PUBLIC OPINION

Despite the wealth of acquisitions, the Musée is still poor in foreign works, and until recently French *avant-garde* art has made only a slow appearance there. What is the cause of this poverty and tardiness? The simple explanation is that every museum reflects the public taste, and that the French public is largely indifferent to the works of foreign artists, and has for too long been hostile to the living art evolving under its eyes between Montmartre and Montparnasse.

It is common knowledge today that the Impressionists were the victims of a truly scandalous persecution. Is it equally recognized or suspected that precisely the same treatment was meted out to their successors? The stupendous prices fetched during the last few years by the canvases of Bonnard, Matisse, Rouault, Picasso, Braque, and the world-wide renown that is now theirs should not obscure the fact that they too, like Manet, Renoir and Gauguin, had for long to meet the most dire hostility. Fauves and Cubists were in their time bitterly scorned. This fact should be kept in mind to explain why, in 1931, no Cubist had a place in the Musée du Luxembourg, no canvas of Dufy, Rouault or Delaunay hung on its walls, and why Bonnard, Matisse, and Utrillo were represented in a niggardly way, and then only by mediocre examples of their work.

As with Impressionism and the movements which followed it, such as the reaction of Cézanne, Gauguin, Van Gogh and Seurat, the painters who formed the fabric of living art after 1890 met at first with nothing but obloquy, insult or scorn. How revealing it is to read the comments of the few critics who deigned to give a line or two to the main forum of these painters, the Salon des Indépendants and the Salon d'Automne! 'It is an orgy, a mad absurdity, an affront to decency, and a monstrous hoax; let there be no mistake, raving lunacy carries the day there.' So complained a commentator who signed himself 'Y' in the *Figaro* of 19th March 1892, writing on the eighth Salon des Indépendants. Maurice Talmeyr, writing in the *Figaro* of 10th May 1895 on the subject of a later Salon, utters woe upon woe. 'There is not a painter today who is capable or can ever be capable of knowing anything but the rapture of private emotion... We can no longer have anything but rambling nonsense and the mad riot of colours we have glimpsed already.' He eloquently entitled his article on the 'cynicism and barn-storming of the present day': 'The bankruptcy of French art'. We hear the same tone, twelve years later, in the *Revue de l'Art Ancien et Moderne*, where Raymond Bouyer, discussing the Salon des Indépendants, exclaims: 'When our young Independents "stutter" under the guise of "decorative synthesis" or a startling "return to style", the masterly stroke of a true draughts-man will remind us, as the poet says: "Form is nothing, but there is nothing without form". Salutary lesson! ... Now that ignorance is pleased to pass itself off as genius, our painters need more than any-thing else the discipline of the craftsman.' To crown this collection of quotations, here are some lines from the *Revue des Beaux-Arts* of 28th December 1913. José Belon, in an article 'Les Ratés célèbres' (Celebrated Failures), berates *avant-garde* artists: 'And so, why have certain Gentlemen once again the effrontery to inflict upon us the empty drivelling of nincompoops and loathsome daubers, whose whole originality consists of a terrific impudence, of a cynicism of the good-for-nothing father's boy safely sheltered from the vicissitudes of fortune?' Remarks in this strain were common currency in the Press from 1890 to 1914; and even today, certain journals and re-views with a 'cultivated and select' public, are not free from similar comments on contemporary *avant-garde* art.

However, we should examine more closely the way in which each of the important movements since 1890 has been judged by its contemporaries. The earliest was the Nabi group. We find Albert Aurier writing enthusiastically about them in the *Mercure de France* of March 1890 and the *Revue Encyclopédique* of 1st April 1892; Lugné Poë discussing in *Art et Critique* an exhibition of their work at Saint-Germain-en-Laye in 1892; and the *Revue Blanche* taking an interest in them; its editors, the Natanson brothers, 'discovered' and defended Vuillard and Bonnard. But these were exceptions; generally the shows of this little group were received with complete silence. There is a typical instance of this attitude in the *Figaro* of 23rd May, 1899, where the art critic Arsène Alexandre, writing of an exhibition of Jongkind's works at the Galerie Durand-Ruel, has not a single word for the Nabi paintings also hanging in the gallery at that time. Like Corot in his time and Redon more recently, the Nabis went almost entirely unnoticed.

We are inclined to be glad of the neglect, when we look back at the disdainful tone of the few notices carried by the Press. 'There can be no excuse for the exclusion of perspective and the suppression of depth, not even the quest for *haute tapisserie*', wrote Alphonse Germain in *La Plume* on 1st September, 1891. The pictures under review were some canvases by Bonnard; one of them, the lovely *Après-midi bourgeoise*, prompted Cochin in the *Gazette des Beaux-Arts* of 1903 to comment: 'In this year 1903, we have a painter, otherwise very accomplished, still playing the old game of shocking the man in the street and making a fool of him. M. Bonnard has given us painting with a light touch and rather ambiguous drawing, all done in a charming grey tint, the "suburban afternoon". We see, depicted with a ferocious joy, slovenly, coarse bourgeois in a setting of the squalid gravelled walks of an ugly little villa near Pantin, or perhaps Aubervilliers.' After hearing this judgment from a shrewd, cultivated man, one who appreciated Bonnard's friend Maurice Denis, it is not surprising to find Henri Revers, editor of the *Revue des Beaux-Arts*, on 16th November, 1913, commenting as follows: 'Some hold that M. Bonnard has great talent, and I would concede that he has some talent. He employs a fine originality in being just himself, but he has no draughtsmanship and his colour he simply borrows from Renoir. What then, remains to him?' Even Maurice Denis, the gentle Denis, whose painting is of a kind to sweeten the sourest of spirits, did not often find favour in the sight of the Zoiluses, the teeth-grinding critics of his time: 'M. Carrière drowns in smoke and fog, but M. Maurice Denis disappears into outer darkness. His *Hommage à Cézanne* brings together nine horribly dressed-up people around an easel, on which is a truly wretched still-life … M. Denis has managed to overstep the limits of abomination. Not a trace of art here – only nothingness, and what is worse, the ridiculous.' So Paul Leroi, writing on the Salon de la Nationale in *Art,* 1901, described one of Denis' most successful canvases.

When a painter as peaceable as Maurice Denis and a movement as temperate as that of the Nabis provoked such acrimony it is not surprising that Fauvism and its exponents should also have roused a violent public protest. Both friends and enemies give a similar account of the stir. Among the friends, we have Michel Puy, brother of the Fauve painter Jean Puy, writing in the *Phalange* of 15th November, 1907, that it was clear to him that the Fauves had 'thoroughly scared the whole of the conservative section of the Salon d'Automne who, after all, are in the majority.' The enemies, for their part, raised a hue and cry. In the *Journal de Rouen* of 20th November 1905, Marcel Nicolle, writing on the subject of the Fauve room in the Salon d'Automne, says: 'We come to the most astounding room in this Salon rich indeed in surprises. Any attempt at description or adequate account or criticism is really impossible, since what is offered to us has – apart from the materials used – no connection with painting. All we get is formless splashes of gaudy colour, blues, reds, yellows, greens, patches of crude colouring jostling together with deplorable effect; these are the uncouth and stupid daubs of a child with a box of paints he has had for Christmas.' This is not to be taken as an expression of opinion by an ignorant provincial behind the times. The daily papers in Paris and the specialist reviews wrote in a similar vein. For J. B. Hall the Fauve room was 'the preserve of pictorial aberration, a mad-house of colours, indescribable fantasies of people who, unless they are having a bit of a joke, should be made to go through the mill at the Ecole des Beaux-Arts.' In *Art et Décoration* of 1906, Camille Mauclair, a critic who enjoyed great authority, wrote: 'A dozen of these Fauves continue, imperturbably, to exhibit their pretentious, ignorant, ludicrous stuff, in which only someone very naïve would see any purpose, even a graceless one.' And time did not reconcile these savage inquisitors to the new heresy in painting.

43

In 1907, in the *Gazette des Beaux-Arts*, André Pératé still thundered against the same Fauves: 'When Monsieur Henri Matisse, Messieurs Othon Friesz, Derain, Braque, Dufy, Czobel exhibited at the Salon de la Libre Esthétique in Brussels, they were placed, quite correctly, in the foreign section. Would that they might keep this classification in Paris; no longer independent but only incoherent, in revolt against the Latin spirit, they mean us to see their distortions as an essential component of the decorative, whereas they leave us merely amazed at an unintentional caricature.'

Each Fauve naturally received his share of blows, but it was Matisse, the ring-leader, by common consent, of this shameful movement, who came off worst. Even some most distinguished critics hung back: Paul Jamot, for instance, although collecting Dufys and Marquets at the time (canvases which he bequeathed to the Musée, and which are its pride today), passed severe judgment in the *Gazette des Beaux-Arts* of 1906: 'There is a room where a few young people surround the disconcerting and versatile M. Matisse who, with his undeniable gifts as a colourist, now goes on to use new methods, apparently to demonstrate his total indifference to reality.' Yet who should cast a stone at this sincere and discriminating critic? In the previous year even André Gide had written, also in the *Gazette des Beaux-Arts:* 'I am willing to admit that Monsieur H. Matisse has extremely fine natural gifts ... The canvases he exhibits today seem to be mere illustrations of his theories. I spent quite a long time in this room. I listened to the remarks of the crowd and, when people cried: "It is quite mad!", I wanted to reply: "Oh no, on the contrary, this is the product of theories ..." Here, everything can be deduced and explained – intuition has no place whatsoever.

'Without a doubt, when Monsieur Matisse paints the forehead of this young woman apple-colour and this tree-trunk pure red, he can say, "It is because ..." Reasonable this painting may be, and it can even be reasoned about by the spectator. How far from the lyric extravagance of a Van Gogh! And from the wings I hear: "Tones must be exaggerated ... the enemy in all painting is grey ... the artist should never be afraid of overstepping the mark."

Yet in the same article in the *Gazette des Beaux-Arts* Gide spoke with admiration of Vuillard, Bonnard and Maillol. And here we put our finger on one of the chief characteristics of contemporary painting, which is that it develops more quickly than criticism, even the best informed. Hardly had the most open-minded, perceptive and subtle critics spoken in defence of a movement and extolled it, than another took its place. Painters and critics moved at a different tempo, and the disparity was even greater between painter and public. This is one of the causes of the gulf that yawns between art and public opinion.

It should be noted that the critics who resist a particular school, tend to accept it when a new one appears on the horizon. To take only two instances: there was André Pératé who wrote of M. Maurice Denis in *Revue de l'Art Ancien et Moderne* of 1897: '... who seems, however, in two of his panels to make outrageous fun of the public,' and who in the *Gazette des Beaux-Arts* of 1907 lauds him as 'a twentieth-century primitive in whom the gift for love vitalises and transforms knowledge.' Again, the critic whose severe strictures on the Fauves we have quoted, on the occasion of the Salon des Indépendants of 1907 (cf *Gazette des Beaux-Arts* vol. I, p. 353 *et seq*) began some months later, when Cubism conducted its first campaign at the Salon d'Automne, to speak of the 'classic simplicity' of Camoin and Manguin, of the 'sobering down' of Matisse and of the 'astonishing force of truth' of Vlaminck (cf vol. II, p. 385). As the saying goes—'one fire drives out another.'

Cubism threw the supporters of the Fauves off balance: Louis Vauxcelles for instance, a supporter of the Fauves, wrote in *Gil Blas* of October 1912, on the Salon d'Automne, 'I would not go as far as Salmon and say that members of the same family fight to the death... for and against these bores, the Cubists. I cannot think this passing craze for pictorial geometry will have world-wide repercussions.' Again, Nourey, the critic of the *Journal*, reporting on the famous Room 41 of the Salon des Indépendants, where the selection committee had brought together a collection of paintings by Delaunay, Marcel Duchamp, Gleizes, Marie Laurencin, La Fresnaye,

Le Fauconnier, Fernand Léger, Metzinger, Picabia and Reth, in addition to sculpture by Archipenko, deplored 'their novelty, which is a return to primitive savagery and barbarism and is, in its essence, a repudiation or a debasing of all the beauties of nature and human life.'

The Impressionists of 1874–1875 had had their share of abuse, but they, at any rate, were not honoured by the attentions of the Conseil Municipal of Paris, of the Chamber of Deputies or the *Journal Officiel* of the French Republic – attentions that speak volumes for the biting hostility encountered by the Cubists. Their full-scale exhibition at the Salon d'Automne of 1912 prompted an open letter from M. Lampué, *doyen* of the Conseil Municipal of Paris, to M. Bérard, Under-secretary of State in the Ministry of Fine Arts, in the following terms: 'If a Municipal Councillor may have your ear, I want to beg you, even implore you, to go the rounds of the Salon d'Automne. Just go, sir, and notwithstanding your being a Minister, I hope you will come out as nauseated as many other people of my acquaintance; I go so far as to hope that you will say to yourself, "Am I abusing my office in consenting to make a public building available to a gang of ruffians who conduct themselves in the world of art like hooligans in everyday life?" You will ask yourself, my dear Minister, on coming out, if nature and the human form have ever been submitted to such outrage; you will be depressed on finding displayed in this Salon the most deplorable ugliness and vulgarity; you will wonder, sir, whether the dignity of the government of which you are a part is not seriously injured, since it seems to give its patronage to such a scandal by providing a roof in a public building for monstrosities such as these.' The Deputy of the Cher, Jean-Louis Breton, put a question to the Under-secretary of State for the Fine Arts in a speech recorded in the *Journal Officiel:* 'I ask the Under-secretary simply to require the Societies who take the premises to give precise guarantees, especially as to the Selection Committee, and to warn them that in future, if the scandal of this year's exhibition is repeated, he would feel obliged to refuse them the Grand Palais. It is indeed ... absolutely unwarranted that our official buildings should be used for shows like these, with a clear anti-art and anti-national character.'

These strictures drew a response from Marcel Sembat who, speaking in defence of Cubism, ended his speech by saying: 'We make no protest when the State lets the official buildings to dubious schemers, to commercial scamps, but we are up in arms when it makes it possible for these artists to exhibit paintings there which are judged to be bad ... When a picture appears to you to be bad, you have an incontestable right – that of not looking at it and going to see others. But we don't call in the police!'

Who can pretend that with himself the era of incomprehension of authentic values in painting has come to an end? Let us admit that every original movement in art seems strange and unpleasing and meets only with censure; it is the same in 1961 as it was in 1874 and 1912. Delacroix complained at the end of his life, and not without cause, that for long he had been 'left to the wolves'. How many Cubist painters and their followers might justly have uttered the same complaint? For each Picasso or Braque who since 1919 has enjoyed renown and sold his canvases at high prices the world over, a multitude of artists have lived in want and worked in obscurity, if not hostility.

One of the greatest treasures of the Musée d'Art Moderne today, Jacques Villon's landscape *Between Toulouse and Albi*, was shown at the Salon d'Automne of 1941 and bought on my suggestion for the sum of 10,000 old francs, the price asked by the artist whom success still eluded, although he was then sixty-six. I also brought to the notice of the Comité des Conservateurs and the Conseil des Musées, in 1950, one of Robert Delaunay's paintings of the *Tour Eiffel*, an enormous composition which was then being used to block up a window in a Paris garage, and which the proprietor was delighted to exchange for the sum of 40,000 old francs. Here we have Robert Delaunay and Jacques Villon, acclaimed today as painters of genius and recognized as of major importance in the history of painting, in 1941 and 1950 still unknown or else dismissed with contempt.

Surrealist and abstract painting met with the same fate as that of the Nabis, the Fauves and the Cubists: the critics and the public were baffled. Perhaps this honours list may be completed with the instance of an independent, one of those geniuses who refuse to be regimented in any school: Rouault. His case serves to demonstrate that the solitary amongst painters is not any better understood than those who subscribe to a coterie. Personality, talent, independence and courage will always horrify the majority of the critics and public. Rouault was a founder of the Salon d'Automne and served in its administration; even so he was not spared a struggle, in company with Piot and Desvallières, against the chairman Francis Jourdain and other members of the management when it came to admitting the Fauves, Matisse in particular. Guillaume Apollinaire describes the scene in *Je sais tout*, 1907: 'Rouault puts his case and quotes the famous rules. He becomes purple in the face and gesticulates at the chairman, who seizes him by the throat with a hand of iron and shakes him like a sapling. "I stand by the rules!" Francis Jourdain shouts, whilst Rouault, locked in his grasp, becomes a deeper purple ... and while the unfortunate Rouault sinks into a chair to catch his breath, they put it to the vote and the *Coiffeuse* of Matisse is refused.' Not surprisingly Rouault's own work was a target for hostility and stupid attacks. Louis

Portrait of the artist as Neptune, 1922, by Kees van Dongen.   ▷
Signed.
Oil on canvas: 170 cm. × 120 cm.

Besides its brilliant qualities as a painting, this work possesses a twofold interest: it preserves for us a likeness of the painter, with all his splendid vitality, at the peak of his success; and it evokes a particular fancy-dress party that he gave at his studio in the rue Juliette Lamber for Paris Society – and the society of Montmartre and Montparnasse – during the reckless years after the 1914–18 war. At this period Society posed for him and applauded, either with masochism or unconsciously, the savage likenesses that Van Dongen recorded of it.

Vauxcelles in *Gil Blas* of 14th October, 1904, describes 'the derisive mob that jostled in front of three or four of his pitch-dark paintings,' and the critic of the *Petit Parisien* of the same date deplores his 'drowning his talent in the exaggeration of reality'. In *Art et Décoration* another critic lashes his palette: 'the strange visions of M. Rouault which unfortunately are lost for everyone in impenetrable blacks.' The critics continued to attack his work savagely throughout 1905, and 1906 saw no abatement of this ferocity, quite the reverse: 'I cannot admire the art in question,' wrote the critic of *L'Univers,* and in *L'Idée* Henri de Pesquidou execrated 'this mass of shrieking colours, often horribly offensive to the eye.' In the *Revue Théâtrale,* Camille Le Senne considers 'horrific, the *Three Graces* escaped from the morgue' that Rouault exhibited at the Salon des Indépendants. The big exhibition of his works in 1910 at the Galerie Druet also made most of the Press critics gang up against him. Even Apollinaire, writing in *L'Intransigeant,* protested: 'I am perturbed by the recklessness of M. Rouault in exhibiting this collection of his nightmares at the Galerie Druet. It is the work of a hack and sad stuff at that.' The unfavourable comments ranged from that of the editor of *Le Témoin,* who wondered 'how a man who has a roof, heating and lighting, is carefree and without fear for the future, can have such black ideas,' to Regis Michaut in the *Revue du Mois* who gave the title 'baptism of chimpanzee' to the fine water-colour now in the Musée d'Art Moderne, *Saint John baptizing Jesus in the Jordan.*

Anyone turning the pages of the contemporary dailies, weeklies, periodicals or reviews, will find innumerable examples of the rage excited by Rouault's masterpieces. Thus it would seem to be inevitable that an Under-secretary of State for the Fine Arts – a man of considerable culture and most civilized taste – refused to purchase for the nation a magnificent picture by Rouault, *Two Nudes,* which the Commission du Musée du Luxembourg proposed to acquire for a ludicrously small sum. In a system where acquisition is guided by public opinion, it could not be otherwise.

The case of Rouault, which has been described, could be echoed in respect of Matisse and Dufy, Picasso and Braque, Léger and Chagall,

Robert Delaunay and Jacques Villon—not to mention the sculptors, even the most classical, such as Maillol and Despiau—Despiau, to whom in 1941 the Académie des Beaux-Arts preferred Lejeune. There is no need then to search further to discover why, up to about 1930, none of the supreme artists of the twentieth century had a place in the Musée du Luxembourg: the principal, not to say sole, reason was the lack of appreciation by the public and the critics, and its compelling influence on those responsible for policy.

There are no grounds for asserting, as many do, that the true values in French art were better appreciated abroad; such a fable does not stand up to the scrutiny of the historian. Take, for instance, the case of Rouault. The foreign Press was far from making a more just estimate of him than our own. The *New York Herald* attacked him in October 1904, March 1906 and March 1908, and in February 1910 took the view that the masterpieces exhibited at the Galerie Druet were 'works that one's intelligence refuses to accept as serious, and that can only be compared with the 'manufactures' of M. Matisse.' That Germany was no more perceptive than the United States is shown by a criticism in the *Pariser Zeitung* of 1st April, 1905. To turn from the particular to the general, there is for example the Armory Show, held in the United States in February 1913, where French art shocked the foreigner just as it had shocked France. Guy Habasque gave an excellent account, in *L'Oeil* of February 1959, of how the Association of American Painters and Sculptors, directed by Arthur B. Davies and encouraged by Walter Pach, Walt Kuhn and Alfred Maurer, put on an international exhibition of modern art, running to about fifteen hundred items, in the barracks of the 69th Infantry Regiment in Lexington Avenue, New York. (These were the only premises large enough to take such a number of canvases, sculptures, water-colours and drawings.)

Subsequently the exhibition moved on to Chicago, and thence to Boston. About half of the exhibits were works of American *avant-garde* painters; the rest were the work of Europeans, for the most part Frenchmen and foreigners of the School of Paris. From Goya, Ingres and Corot to Rodin, Cézanne, Redon, Gauguin and Van

Gogh, the art of the nineteenth century was superbly represented. There was nothing there that could come as a revelation or shock to the New York public, already familiar with Impressionism. However, it was otherwise with the Fauves, the Cubists and the artists influenced by Cubism. Despite several exhibitions organised since 1908 by the photographer Alfred Stieglitz in his gallery at 291, Fifth Avenue, they remained practically unknown to the average American. Twenty-one works by Rouault, eleven canvases by Matisse, contributions by Derain, Vlaminck, Marquet and Dufy, showed Fauvism at its most brilliant; and seven Picassos, three Braques, two works of Gleizes, two of Léger, five of La Fresnaye, eight Villons, four by Marcel Duchamp, four by Picabia and three Delaunays[1] provided a carefully selected cross-section of Cubism, Orphism and the *Section d'Or.*

As to sculpture, there were exhibits by Bourdelle and Maillol, while Raymond Duchamp-Villon, Brancusi and Archipenko were represented by some of their main works.

Immediately there came an explosion of mirth and a burst of indignation. The clamour provoked by the Matisses and Picassos was mild, however, compared with that which greeted Marcel Duchamp, Picabia and Brancusi, whose respective paintings, *Nude descending a staircase, Procession in Seville,* and *Mademoiselle Pogany,* were taken to be signs of dementia brought on by the pursuit of novelty. The American critics showed no more understanding than those of France; and we are told on good authority that in Chicago students burnt Matisse, Brancusi and Walter Pach in effigy.

How many of the several hundred thousand visitors whom the scandal brought to the Armory Show in New York, and those, no less numerous, who came to the International Exhibition in Chicago and Boston, appreciated that they had before them a fair number of masterpieces which had already given a new direction to art? Very

[1] Two only were exhibited, and shortly afterwards Delaunay, annoyed that his *City of Paris* had not been hung – for the reason or on the pretext that it was outsize – withdrew all the pictures he had sent.

few, no doubt, although about 250 works found buyers, and a handful of connoisseurs like Barnes, Arensberg, Arthur Jerome Eddy, Miss Lillie Bliss, 'saw the light' and made their first purchases, the nucleus of their subsequent famous collections.

All the artists of the last decade of the nineteenth century and the beginning of the twentieth were at first obscure, then not understood, then began to attract the interest of a quite small circle of connoisseurs, French and foreign, mostly perceptive critics, discerning amateurs and dealers with a flair. Thus Bonnard attracted the attention about 1892 of Albert Aurier, Félix Fénéon and the contributors to the *Revue Blanche*, the dealers Barc de Boutteville and Ambroise Vollard, the French collector Thadée Natanson, and the Swiss connoisseurs, M. and Mme Hahnloser of Winterthur. In the same way, Matisse, spotted by Michel Puy, Marcel Sembat, the Russian Shchukin and the Americans Gertrude and Leo Stein, came to rouse the interest of directors of galleries – Ambroise Vollard and the Bernheim brothers. It is the same story with the Cubists. The majority of writers in the Press attacked them but they were defended, more or less discreetly, in the *avant-garde* reviews such as the *Revue de France et des pays français, Montjoie, Soirées de Paris, Revue Indépendante, Durandal, Revue d'Europe et d'Amérique*, and also by André Salmon on the staff of *Paris Journal* and by Apollinaire, art critic of *L'Intransigeant*. The dealers had an inkling of their talent – Clovis Sagot, Vollard and especially Kahnweiler, and so had the writers, Jacques Rivière in particular. Some connoisseurs also approved – Frenchmen like Roger Dutilleul, Henri-Pierre Roché, Alexandre Marcereau and Granier the attorney; Americans like the Steins, the two Cones, Walter Pach; Russians such as Shchukin and Germans such as Wilhelm Uhde. This then was the start of the journey towards recognition, to quote Beaumarchais – 'a faint sound, a rumour, skimming the ground like swallows before the storm.' It was a rumour which swelled, spread, and finished as 'the rising acclaim of the public, a world-wide chorus' of praise and admiration. The relentless enemies who dogged their beginnings became the most extravagant enthusiasts, the journalists who at first were most hostile now wrote only eulogies.

During the period between obscurity and acclaim, what were the private galleries about? The procedure is generally for the painter to enter into a contract with the gallery; the form may vary but in general it goes in this way: the artist assigns the whole of his work to the gallery for a stated period against an undertaking that he receive monthly remittances according to his success, the number of his exhibits, the dimensions of the works, etc. The advantage for the artist in such contracts is obvious; he is assured of his daily bread, sometimes even of a comfortable living, and becomes in a manner of speaking an employee who has only to go and draw his pay at the end of the month. His anguished search for a purchaser for his work is over. Gone also, the pursuit of a critic or a review to give it a notice. All this now falls on the dealer. The artist can work in tranquillity, and he is well aware that security of this kind is worth having, though admitting that the dealer sells his works at two or three times the figure he has paid him for them.

However, there is another side to the coin: first, the artist is financially at the mercy of his gallery, which can 'sink' him from one day to the next, if he gets on bad terms with the dealer, by throwing a whole bundle of his works on the market and turning them into cash at an absurd figure. There are several instances of painters who have never recovered from such unfortunate experiences. And then, the artist does sign away some of his individual and creative freedom. The lawsuit which Rouault brought against the heirs of Ambroise Vollard has been so much aired and discussed that there is no need to go into it again here. Every human action is fraught with risk and that of the artist who ties himself to the dealer is no exception to the rule.

It is only too true that to bring his name before the public at large, the artist must almost always be beholden to a dealer. Jacques Villon, for instance, fervently admired within his own coterie in the years 1941–1944, only reached the world-wide public to which his genius entitled him when one of the galleries took his interests in hand. However, besides the fact that a dealer is seldom the first to discover an artist, there may be many set-backs in the attempts of a gallery to launch him. Early in this century the exhibition rooms of a certain famous dealer were full, it is said, of canvases by Degas, Renoir, Cézanne and Gauguin which he had bought when no one was interested in them; but the tale adds that his cellar was stuffed with works by Charlot and Jacqueline Marval! Many a painting will not sell in spite of publicity. In the final analysis, the deciding factor is talent – this is what opened the doors of the Musée du Luxembourg and later of the Musée d'Art Moderne to all the gifted and original artists of the School of Paris of the last decade of the nineteenth century and the sixty years of this one.

THE NEW ATTITUDE TOWARDS CONTEMPORARY ART

We cannot here attempt a detailed analysis of the events that enabled the Musée d'Art Moderne to march with the times and to welcome *avant-garde* art, both that of the first half of the twentieth century, which has already passed into history, and that being evolved in Paris by artists now aged between thirty and fifty. But a few remarks upon this change of attitude – which to a large extent was influenced by and reflected public opinion – will not be out of place.

In the first place, the French State is no longer bound fast to the institutions given to it by Napoleon I. True the State had made a half-hearted attempt in 1863 to free itself from them, but they had survived successive régimes and imposed on France an art which was lifeless and academic in the extreme. Today, moreover, the Institut de France, the Salon des Artistes Français and the Prix de Rome no longer enjoy the power and prestige which made it possible for eighteen members of the Académie des Beaux-Arts to protest in 1896 against the exhibition of the Caillebotte Bequest at the Musée du Luxembourg. Nor could they appoint as chairman of the Conseil Supérieur des Beaux-Arts such a man as Léon Bonnat, so bitter an adversary of his former pupil Toulouse-Lautrec that in 1905 he persuaded the Conseil to refuse twice over the gift of Lautrec's *Portrait of M. Delaporte,* now a pride of the Copenhagen Museum. Nowadays a far bolder spirit informs our institutions. Henri-Georges Adam, for instance, teaches sculpture at the École des Beaux-Arts, and the Académie de France in Rome has just been placed under the direction of Balthus. And there have been attempts to submit the entries of the candidates for the Prix de Rome to the arbitration of artists such as Chastel, Estève, Masson, Schneider, Singier and Soulages. The time is past when the Institut, the École des Beaux-Arts and the Salon des Artistes Français governed the artistic life of France and could shut the doors of the Luxembourg to Manet, Renoir, Cézanne, Gauguin, and later to Rouault and Braque, whilst opening them to Gérôme, Bonnat, Jean-Paul Laurens, and then to Cottet, Besnard and Jacques-Émile Blanche, the three painters most liberally represented in the Musée du Luxembourg before 1930, by ten, seven, and six works respectively. The State, no longer bound hand and foot by its institutions and healthily sceptical about them after long experience, liberal and encouraging to all trends, even the boldest, is no longer fearful of declaring through the mouth of a Minister that the important art of today is non-figurative, nor of purchasing and exhibiting in the Musée d'Art Moderne the most challenging works in sculpture and painting.

The reason for this change in policy is that the State feels it has the sanction of public opinion. In 1916 fifty-six Deputies could without fear of ridicule vote that Rodin's bequest of the works in his studio be refused. And while it is true that a *Société pour l'Esthétique Générale* de la France protested and brought an action against Le Corbusier for his splendid structure at the gates of Marseilles, nowadays such happenings are rare. I know of no voice raised against the building of Le Corbusier at Nantes, nor against his church at Ronchamp – one of the supreme achievements of the art of the twentieth century. Although still not highly enlightened, the taste of the public is now better educated; this can be seen in the numerous and usually well chosen exhibitions put on by provincial towns either for the education of their inhabitants or – still more significantly – to attract tourists. People came and continue to come in throngs to visit, for instance, the church on the Plateau d'Assy or the Dominican chapel decorated by Matisse at Vence, two achievements which speak volumes for the artistic education both of the Christian laity and the clergy – brought about by two great encouragers of sacred art, the reverend fathers Couturier and Regamey.

The public now owes its information and education partly to the activities of private organizations such as the *Amis de l'Art*, and of official bodies such as the *Service Educatif des Musées Nationaux*, which arranges visits of school-children to the museums under the guidance of a well-informed personnel, provides many exhibitions of original works as well as reproductions in museums, lycées, colleges, schools, etc. in the provinces,–and partly to the cinema and television. The viewing public has been introduced to Odilon Redon and Rouault, for instance, on the excellent television programmes by Jean-Marie Drot, while the cinema has contributed such short films as *Jérôme Bosch* by Luciano Emer, and *Van Gogh* by Alain Resnais, and a long film, the fine *Mystère Picasso* by Clouzot.

Nowadays reproductions of modern art have an ever-increasing circulation. Colour postcards, colour prints, lavish and faithful to the original, books splendidly illustrated in colour, find their way into the hands of a growing public. According to a bookseller in Paris, whereas before the war there was no sale for illustrated books on the history of art, these now provide one of his best-selling lines, and books on contemporary art are in the majority. Modern homes have colour prints on the walls, often reproductions of extremely modern abstract paintings. This revival of interest in the visual–perhaps due to the growth of the cinema, television, photography, illustrated periodicals and books, posters, publicity leaflets and so on,–is found the world over. In Germany, in the United States and especially in Japan, vast crowds press into art exhibitions. More than a hundred thousand Japanese in six weeks went to see the exhibition of French art organised in Tokyo in 1954. And in 1953 in Los Angeles the retrospective Rouault exhibition drew more than three times as many visitors as it had done in Paris the previous year. It should be noted too in this connection, that the peak months for the Musée d'Art Moderne are those when foreign tourists are in Paris. Today the foreign public is certainly more interested than the French in art, and perhaps especially in contemporary French art.

Paris has become, since 1919, the principal market for modern painting, drawing buyers of all nationalities. At the same time, the number of foreign artists living in Paris is continually swelled by newcomers. Of the seventy thousand artists at present at work between Montmartre and Montparnasse, about a third were born elsewhere than in France and have come from regions as far apart as Scandinavia and the Argentine, Canada and Korea, India and Venezuela,

Israel and Cuba, Poland and South Africa. Many of them live in direst poverty, but their ardour cannot be damped.

With this still mounting number of artists, the galleries too multiply. It has become more difficult to launch a painter and his work, but the technique devised at the beginning of the century has been skilfully brought up to date. Some galleries publish or subsidise reviews and periodicals which naturally refrain from unfavourable criticism of works the gallery exhibits. Others publish expensively-produced catalogues. Others again, aiming at a wealthier public, offer prospective patrons on opening day a generous buffet with champagne and whisky on tap. Many have links with 'opposite numbers' in various cities abroad, and keep in friendly touch with them. But all this boosting will be in vain unless it is on behalf of an artist of undeniable talent.

Conversely, talent is assured of eventual success; as Apollinaire, with his poet's perception, said of the Cubists: 'Those who deride the new painters deride their own image, for the men of the future will get their impression of the men of today from the representations of him that the painters of the most living art, that is the newest, will have left behind them.'

It is the aim of the Conservateurs that the Musée d'Art Moderne shall reflect our times, showing them in their true perspective, and that it shall be the museum of the twentieth century. Well aware though they are that all human achievement must fall short of the ideal, they nevertheless hope that in what they offer to the public, the gap between the splendid design and its fulfillment shall not be too evident.

THE PLATES

PAUL SIGNAC (1863–1935)
Port of Marseilles

1911
Oil on canvas
Height 125 cm. (49″)
Width 135 cm. (53¹/₂″)

Signac, together with Seurat, was the founder of Neo-Impressionism, the experiments of which he charted in his well-known book *D'Eugène Delacroix au Néo-Impressionisme*, and he remained faithful to the art of his youth during his whole lifetime. In this particular school, certain elements derive from Impressionism, such as the bright colour, the touch based on Divisionism, the desire to communicate the luminous atmosphere and the feeling for all aspects of nature in movement – of water especially, and it is this last that has made Signac the supreme painter of the sea-ports of France and the Mediterranean. But in other respects Signac's painting differs from that of Monet: as far as the chromatism is concerned, the laws of contrast and of the complementary are applied – no longer empirically as with Monet, but with method; the treatment also is far more systematic, for the Impressionists' 'commas', used freely, are replaced by regular dots of a calculated size.

At complete variance with the spontaneous lay-out dear to the Impressionist group, the composition is very studied. Here it is based on a precise screen of verticals and horizontals, where depth is suggested by diagonals and movement is provided by segments of curves (sails and sterns of ships). In this way Signac satisfies the impulse for decoration that he has in common with all the painters of his generation, such as Seurat, Gauguin and Toulouse-Lautrec.

This canvas is characteristic of Signac's experiments throughout his career. It is an especially good example of his work during the second part of his life, when he gave up the rather soft colour-scale of his youth for one of far greater vigour and intensity.

Shown at the Salon des Indépendants, 1911 (No. 5638). Purchased by the State 1912. Musée du Luxembourg.

HENRI-EDMOND CROSS (1856–1910)   Signed
LES ILES D'OR   Oil on canvas
                                                         Height 60 cm. (23$^1/_2$")
                                                          Width 55 cm. (21$^1/_2$")

This painting was acquired by the Musées Nationaux at the First Fénéon
Sale on 30 April, 1947. It is well known that Fénéon was a connoisseur of
Neo-Impressionist work, and he was a close friend of Seurat, Signac and
Cross. The artist, with Signac, ranks next after Seurat as the most distinguished of the Neo-Impressionist group, and this particular canvas is one
of the most striking of his works. Here we have the window giving on the
open-air scene, a slice of landscape arbitrarily cut (to the frame of the
window), without any hint of an artificial lay-out. It illustrates how much
the Neo-Impressionists strove after luminosity; they persisted too in preserv-
ing in their paintings an image of the atmosphere. In this twofold aim there
is proof of their realism, and this picture has perhaps never been surpassed
as an expression of it. More than that, it shows the quest for style and the
will to order and discipline which marks off the Neo-Impressionists from
Impressionism. At the same time it clearly reveals the personality of Cross
in the exquisite subtlety of his colour and the deftness of execution. The
picture proves the influence of a movement and also of an artist whose
effect tends today to be overlooked. For instance a *View of the Thames,*
painted by Derain about 1906, is an admission that the Fauves had cast
a look in the direction of Cross and had admired the boldness of his compositions which, like this of the *Iles d'Or,* dispense with any solid plane
but are stepped in depth and get the effect of solidity with nothing more
than empty spaces – empty beach, empty sea, empty sky.

EMILE BERNARD (1868–1941)   1887, signed and dated
STONEWARE JUG AND APPLES   Oil on canvas
Height 46 cm. (18″)   Width 55 cm. (21¹/₂″)
Before Bernard started to model himself on the sixteenth-century Venetian
masters in 1895 he had been, when he was twenty, much in the company of
Toulouse-Lautrec and Signac, Van Gogh, Gauguin and Cézanne. He was a
pioneer of the avant-garde at the time he painted this picture, inscribed on
the back 'First attempt in synthetism and simplification, 1887'. He turned
from the Impressionists but retained their colour-range. He replaced Impressionist analysis, breaking up the form, by a simplifying 'synthesis'. Here
the influence of Cézanne was decisive as the apples, modelled by colour and
not by tonal values, prove. The outline round them evokes the art of Gauguin who, it may be, only came to 'synthesis' under the influence of Bernard.
Again, the decided, conspicuous brush strokes have something in common
with those of Van Gogh. Purchased by the Musées Nationaux in 1953.

PAUL SERUSIER (1865–1927)
Little Breton girl, seated

1895, signed
Oil on canvas
Height 92 cm. (36¹/₄″)
Width 54 cm. (21¹/₄″)

During the autumn of 1888 at Pont-Aven Sérusier was converted by Gauguin to 'synthesis', and he went on to preach it at the Académie Julian, where he got the support of a little group of his fellow-students who called themselves the 'Nabis' after a Hebrew word meaning prophet. The art of the Nabis, and of Sérusier in particular, owes much to Gauguin; the debt is easily seen in this picture – which must certainly be identified with No. 1390 in the catalogue of the Salon des Indépendants of 1895 – '*Portrait of Marie*, property of M. Thadée Natanson.' Here we have the Breton subject,

MAURICE DENIS (1870–1943)
THE MUSES

1893, signed and dated
Oil on canvas
Height 168 cm. (66")
Width 135 cm. (53")

It was Maurice Denis who set out the theory of the Nabi Group in his writings, and this canvas is a typical example of Nabi experiment. He was influenced by Puvis de Chavannes and his famous *Sacred Grove,* and therefore, like Sérusier, he aims at the decorative style. He achieves this for the most part in five ways: he dispenses with perspective, superimposes planes, abhors any empty spaces, lifts the horizon, brings life into the still zones by means of detail; uses stylization – especially of line, but also of form – one is aware of this in the drawing of the leaf shadows and in the treatment of the tree-trunks and figures. This stylizing goes with simplification of contours stressed by the outlines, of colour spread in unbroken surfaces, and with the flattening of masses – all features which prove how much Denis owes to Gauguin. But his originality breaks through in the highly descriptive manner of his drawing, at once taut and flowing, typical of *art nouveau,* and in the languor and rather excessive affectedness of the figures (this is the period of Maeterlinck and of Symbolism), as well as in its tender poetry.

At the Salon des Indépendants, 1893 (No. 366). Collection of A. Fontaine. Purchased by the Musées Nationaux at the A. Fontaine sale, 1932.

Continued from page 65

simplification of line, of tone and form, contour stressed by an outline, colour spread flat, disregard of perspective, flattening of the figure and the painter's decorative aims perceptible in his use of the hieratic and archaic. On the other hand, the preference for a harmony in a minor key with greys and blacks as a basis, the effort to get a matt quality, and thin dry paint, with a touch of humour added, distinguish this canvas from those of Gauguin and relate it to those of the other Nabis.

At the Salon des Indépendants, 1895 (No. 1390). Thadée Natanson collection. Madame Thadée Natanson collection. Bequeathed by Mme Thadée Natanson, 1953.

MAURICE DENIS (1870–1943)
Homage to Cézanne
1900, signed and dated
Oil on canvas
Height 180 cm. (71″). Width 240 cm. (94¹/₂″)

Just as Fantin-Latour had painted a *Homage
to Delacroix* in 1864, so in 1900 Maurice
Denis was moved to express the admiration
he and his fellow-Nabis felt for Cézanne,
who was then just emerging from obscurity.
Around a Cézanne still-life he brought together a number of Nabis: Sérusier, who
is commenting on the picture, Ranson, who
had opened a school for teaching the Nabi
theory of aesthetics, K. X. Roussel and
Bonnard on the right, and Vuillard on the
left. Denis himself is in the background next
to Sérusier. Besides the painters, he has
brought in his wife (on the extreme right),
the dealer Vollard, whose shop is the setting
for the scene, and also the art critic Mellerio.

This *Homage to Cézanne* is also homage
to Odilon Redon, seen on the extreme left,
the sole painter of the earlier generation to
whom Denis' friends and fellow artists
opened their ranks. Redon left remarkable
portraits of Bonnard, Vuillard, Denis and
Sérusier, who so often and so eagerly used
to turn up in his salon – drawn there by
immense admiration for his art and his informed taste, as well as for his intellect and
goodness of heart.

And then again it is a homage to Gauguin, venerated by the Nabis. Denis perhaps
chose this of all Cézanne's canvases because it had belonged to Gauguin,
who set especial store by it. 'The Cézanne', he wrote to Schuffenecker
in 1888, 'is a pearl of price and I have already refused an offer of
300 francs. It is the apple of my eye and unless I am driven by dire
necessity I shall part with my last shirt before yielding it.' Cézanne, Redon,

Gauguin: these with Puvis de Chavannes, the Japanese print, the tapestries of the fifteenth century and Breton folk art, were the most potent influence on Nabi painting and decisively set its course towards the subjective image and the decorative. When *Homage to Cézanne* was exhibited with great acclaim at the Salon de la Nationale in 1900, it was bought by Gide, that

ARISTIDE MAILLOL (1861–1944)
LA FEMME A L'OMBRELLE

c. 1895–1900, signed
Oil on canvas
Height 193 cm. (76″)
Width 149 cm. (58¹/₂″)

Although Maillol is famous the world over as a sculptor, he began as a painter, a Nabi and a believer in their theory of aesthetics. This comes to mind at once in looking at this picture, where he ignores traditional perspective, raises the horizon, avoids giving a third dimension, and seeks the decorative effect which at that time he was also pursuing in tapestries. Like the Nabis, his models are Gauguin, Puvis de Chavannes and the painters of the Italian Quattrocento especially: from them he borrows the profile representation and stylized treatment, as well as the very defined and elegant linearism of his style. There is no hint here of the future sculptor: the form is scarcely modelled and Maillol shows himself above all an exquisite colourist and composer of sensitive harmonies. By the exactness of the tone as well as the tremor of the touch, the painter makes a breath of luminous air quiver in the canvas, proving that he was not as blind to the Impressionist pictures as he was sometimes said to be.

In the Farraill Collection, Nancy; Maillol Exhibition, Musée des Beaux-Arts, Nancy, March 1953 (No. 9). Purchased by the Musées Nationaux, 1955.

Continued from page 69

fervent admirer of Nabi art and of Maurice Denis in particular, who had illustrated his *Voyage d'Urien* in 1893. We see clearly here the spiritual kinship between the essential inspiration of the Nabis and the ebbing tide of Symbolism. Gide himself offered this picture to the Musée du Luxembourg in 1928, whence it passed to the Musée d'Art Moderne.

EDOUARD VUILLARD (1868–1940)
The Gardens of Paris

1894, signed and dated
Tempera on canvas, three panels
Height 213 cm. (84″)   Width 73 cm. (28³/₄″)
213 cm. (84″)   163 cm. (64¹/₂″)
213 cm. (84″)   81 cm. (32″)

The Nabis were championed almost from the first by the *Revue Blanche*, under the direction of Thadée Natanson. It was one of his brothers, Alexandre, who commissioned Vuillard in 1894 to decorate the dining-room of his town house in the Avenue du Bois. The ten panels are today scattered among various galleries (Brussels, Cleveland, Houston etc.), but in 1929 the Musées Nationaux purchased the main panel and the two that flanked it. Their theme is the Gardens of Paris, interpreted very freely with no attempt at realism, and in a mood where light irony is closely welded with the decorative intention. However, beneath are trains of thought that show an extreme revolutionary boldness and range. To begin with, Vuillard, following Degas and influenced by Japanese prints, rejects the principles of composition that have governed Western art since the end of the Middle Ages. He does not place his main group in the middle of the canvas nor does he use symmetrical groups to give counterbalance on either flank. His aim, on the contrary, is a displacement of the true centre, asymmetry, and unbalance; the work is saved from a tilt to the left by compensating for the number of figures on that side by other elements, such as the splashes of sunlight on the ground and the leaves in the curtain of foliage. To achieve this the figures have to be given no more weight or importance than the splashes of light or the leaves: both the one and the other must be no more than elements of this composition as a whole, which the painter treats architecturally. This means that here the human person loses the privileged position it has had in painting since the Renaissance with its emphasis on humanism; that painting

divests itself of its 'anthropocentric' quality, as do learning and philosophy, also, in our time.

The way is now open to an art from which the human figure will be entirely absent – an abstract art, one of the true sources of which we can trace to the Nabis.

Commissioned by Alexandre Natanson. Alexandre Natanson Sale. Purchased by the Musées Nationaux in 1929.

EDOUARD VUILLARD (1868–1940) 1891, signed and dated
AU LIT Oil on canvas

Height 74 cm. (29¹/₈″)

Width 92 cm. (36¹/₄″)

The familiar theme of this painting, treated with a certain irony, reflects
the taste of the Nabis for a domestic intimism and a light touch. Rejection
of depth and modelling indeed produce the 'flat surface covered with
colours brought together in a certain order', the definition to which Maurice
Denis reduced paintings as early as 1892, and to which most of the modern
schools were to hold so fervently. In its simplified geometric drawing it
derives from the aim at 'synthesis'. The function of the discreet colour is
less related to the art of portrayal than to music (a *berceuse* perhaps).

Continued on page 82

EDOUARD VUILLARD (1868–1940)   1906
PORTRAIT OF CLAUDE BERNHEIM DE VILLERS
Oil on paper pasted on cardboard panel
Height 68 cm. (26³/₄")
Width 96 cm. (37³/₄")

That this painting belongs to Vuillard's Nabi period is clear from the
originality of the pose, the boldness of the composition (note on the left
the woman's figure cut by the frame), and, still more, from the deliberate
attempt to obscure easy understanding of the picture – a means of avoiding
a decorative effect. At the same time it has many divergent features. First
it is a portrait, a *genre* to which Vuillard, under pressure of success, was
to devote himself more exclusively, and which drew him towards a realism
that became ever more traditional. Then this work is less simplified than
anything he had done previously. Evident here are Vuillard's new taste
for analysis which was to drive him to heap up detail and incidental
features, and his entirely new interest in light, bringing him to alter his
technique. He puts aside painting with size, spirit-thinned paint or tempera,

75

EDOUARD VUILLARD (1868–1940)   1900, signed and dated
PORTRAIT OF FELIX VALLOTTON IN HIS STUDIO
Tempera on cardboard mounted on panel
Height 65 cm. (25^1/$_2$″)
Width 50.3 cm. (19^1/$_2$″)

Vallotton, a Swiss from Lausanne, was first influenced by the objective realism of Holbein, who inspired his early paintings. In 1882 he went to Paris and through his friend Maurin met the painter Charles Cottet, who in turn introduced him to the Nabis. One of his compositions (inspired by Fantin-Latour's group-portraits, such as *Manet's Studio*) brings together Cottet and Vuillard, Bonnard, Denis and himself. The art of the Nabis had a most happy effect on him: it drew him away from his rather photographic realism, gave him a new regard for style and released his subjective inspiration, sprung from an often caustic irony. He is perhaps at his best during his association with them and before he returned in about 1914 to a more traditional approach and greater realism. Still, he retained his taste for the style he had acquired with the Nabis. Among his Nabi friends was Vuillard, who painted this portrait in Vallotton's flat at 6, rue de Milan. The portrait is sensitive and masterly in execution: the delicacy of the minor tones which he likes so much is lit up by the subtlety of a filtered light – a feature that then began to engross him. The perfect achievement of the composition is based on the contrast between the modulated contour of the silhouette and the simplicity of the rectangular frame hanging in the background. The style, quietly decorative, given by the flattening out of the figure, is extremely pleasing, and so too is the background with its skilfully disposed motifs. The execution, swift and suited with care to the subject, shows his craftman's integrity and artistic devotion. The portrait was a bequest of Carle Dreyfus, 1953.

Continued from page 75

and takes to oils as being more transparent and a better medium for interpreting the play of light on objects. And with that, he has modified his colour-scale, and in this canvas has composed an inimitably beautiful symphony of whites touched with silver and gold, heightened by a few notes of rose and red. Presented by M. and Mme Gaston Bernheim de Villers, 1951.

PIERRE BONNARD (1867–1947)   c. 1892, signed
THE PEIGNOIR   Oil on velvet
                                           Height 154 cm. (60¹/₂″)
                                           Width 54 cm. (21¹/₄″)

From the time Japan became open to Western influence in 1858, her art
took artists and lovers of art in France by storm. Writers such as Baudelaire
and the Goncourts, engravers like Braquemond and painters such as Manet,
Degas and Claude Monet passionately admired the prints of the Ukiyo-e.
Their influence on Manet's painting is obvious, and he acknowledged it by
introducing the figure of a *samurai* in the background of his *Portrait of
Zola*. Degas, too, owes to them the unexpectedness of his settings and his
interpreting of distance by the opposing of two diagonals. Monet borrows
from Hokusai the idea of sequences on a single theme. The leaders of the
reaction against Impressionism in their turn called for lessons in the Japanese
method; Gauguin, Van Gogh and Toulouse-Lautrec all profited by its
elliptic drawing and its skill in using 'still patches' or unfilled spaces; the
Nabis shared the Japanese craze of their forerunners and were greatly
affected by an exhibition of Japanese art that opened in April 1890, at
the Ecole des Beaux Arts. The greatest enthusiast of them all was Bonnard,
who was called the 'Japanese Nabi' by his fellow artists. This painting,
then, is an avowal of his enthusiasm. It is in fact an adaptation of the
kakemonos – in the material on which it is painted, the format, and the
very subject itself. The style, extreme in its synthesis, is Japanese in feeling;
so, too, is the decorative intention, clearly seen in the treatment of the
garment and in the introduction (lower right) of plants that recall the reeds
so common in Japanese painting. Even the signature is inspired by Japanese
characters. Bonnard's originality nevertheless remains unimpaired and is
perceptible in the playfulness with which he treats his theme. Apparently
he painted this work in 1892 when his Japanese manner was most pro-
nounced (his *Checkered bodice* is of the same date). This is a year before
Maurice Denis, inspired too by the *kakemonos* and by the *Peignoir* of his
friend, painted his ravishing *Portrait of Mme Ranson*.

Formerly in the Philippe Bernard Collection. Purchased by the Musées
Nationaux, 1939.

PIERRE BONNARD (1867–1947)
WOMAN DOZING ON A BED

1899, signed
Oil on canvas
Height 96 cm. (37³/₄″)
Width 105 cm. (41¹/₂″)

This painting is one of Bonnard's highest achievements and also, strangely enough, one of his early works, done in 1899, when the artist had not yet discovered, under the influence of the Impressionists, the resources of his brilliant chromatism. At this time he was still taken up with harmonising tones and was content to execute kinds of *camaïeux* (or monochromes), as in the picture *Women and Children*, also of 1899, and to reconcile one or two tones at once close and contrasted, that attract and repel each other. In this large canvas the whites tinged with gold of the bed and of the nude are, so to speak, assailed by dark tones, which here verge on yellow and there even pass over into green. So we have two scales of colour only, and when these are in contrast the harmony reaches a point of perfection (especially as here and there tones of entirely different colour fuse), making the other tones (such as the blue of the cat's neck-bow) vibrate all the more.

Bonnard is an astonishing virtuoso in colour, but at the same time he shows a matchless gift for 'managing' composition, for devising arabesques and interpreting shapes. How striking the lay-out of this painting is: using for the first time a process that he never afterwards forsook (an example is the *Corner of the Table*, page 84), the artist views the subject from above with the effect of tilting the shapes towards the top of the canvas and filling the whole picture space. Remarkable, too, is the rhythm of the lines which spring from the lower left corner and rise fanwise towards the upper right, carried upwards in such a soaring movement that we forget anything of *art nouveau* that may lurk in these floral curves. One of these lines defines the nude woman reclining on the bed – a figure of an incisiveness and a flowering grace, such as Bonnard was to equal in later work but never surpass. Of all his nudes, this is one of the most concise, most lithe and most living. It is also one of the most surprising. The name of Bonnard evokes at once a whole world of enchantment, of light sensuality, of mockery where flirtatious young women busy themselves charmingly with their toilet, exchanging the while witty, unselfconscious remarks. There is nothing of that in this picture. On the contrary, there is an immense fervour and a sensuality that is uneasy and rather agitated, as well as an indefinable aura of the perverse that recalls Goya's *Nude Maja*. An atmosphere of drama pervades it – the drama of desire, of sensual pleasure and of passion as invincible as death and just as tragic. As in other canvases painted

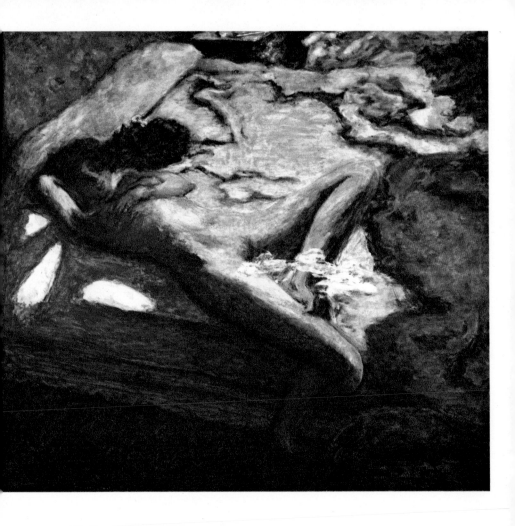

during this period with the same model (the strangest being perhaps *Man and Woman*), Bonnard has here let certain unusual aspects of his genius come to the surface and has proved at the same time that a painter who is truly great can always reach beyond his own limits.

The painting was in the Alexandre Natanson collection; the Alexandre Natanson sale (No. 87); the Félix Fénéon collection; the second Fénéon sale, 1947 (Catalogue No. 67). Purchased by the Musées Nationaux.

PIERRE BONNARD (1867–1947) 1928, signed
PORTRAIT OF REINE NATANSON AND MARTHE BONNARD Oil on canvas
Height 73 cm. (28³/₄″)
Width 57 cm. (22¹/₂″)

Reine Natanson was the second wife of Thadée Natanson, the former editor of the *Revue Blanche* and a close friend of Bonnard, about whom he wrote a book, *Le Bonnard que je propose*. She sat several times for Bonnard, especially in 1920 and 1921, but the finest of these portraits is that of 1928, in which she posed for the artist with Marthe Bonnard. The dress she is wearing appears also in another painting in the Musée d'Art Moderne, the *Red bodice*, of 1925. There is a striking contrast between the red dress with white stripes and the yellow one of the other sitter – and a contrast equally impressive between the background flooded with light and the foreground in the shadows cast by the foliage of a tree. By these means Bonnard gives an unparalleled radiance to the colour and at the same time succeeds in introducing into this glow something strangely enigmatic: it is expressed, too, in a hint of languor that gives a dreaming look to the face of Marthe Bonnard and in the metamorphosis which his original angle of vision applies to the cat seen in the background and the fruit in the foreground. It seems inevitable to apply to Bonnard the words used so aptly by Barrès to define the *genre* of Claude Lorrain – 'mystery seen in the full light of day'.

In the collection of Thadée Natanson. Collection of Mme Thadée Natanson. Bequest of Mme Thadée Natanson, 1953.

Continued from page 74

Especially noticeable is the very bold distortion of the figure, elongated as if to form the curve of a garland. Its central sag suggests the complete lassitude of body and mind in sleep and shows that Vuillard prefers expressiveness of form to anatomical accuracy – in this anticipating the German Expressionists. The band in the upper part of the canvas, meant only to balance another band below formed by the carpet, bears out that for the Nabis, even then, the picture was above all a construction hingeing on 'plastic rhythms', rather than an image of the material world. Vuillard Donation, 1941.

PIERRE BONNARD (1867–1947)
CORNER OF THE TABLE

1935, signed
Oil on canvas
Height 67 cm. (26¹/₂″)
Width 63,5 cm. (25″)

Everything in this superlative work of Bonnard deserves close attention. The view from above adjusts the plane of the table to make it coincide with the picture plane. This allows the artist, still held in his later years by certain likes and dislikes of his youth, to avoid a traditional perspective that hollows the picture. Instead, he is free to accentuate the two-dimensional character of his work and thus bring out an extremely decorative effect, one that is wholly mural in feeling. The close-up view of the objects on the table not only gives them a strange and hence poetic look, but allows Bonnard a chance to pass over the things that are of no interest to him (such as the chair on the upper left). At the same time it allows him to emphasize and magnify the fruit in the foreground so as to increase the more its symbolism of prodigal Nature. The colour, too, contributes to this enhancement. Two hot tones – a vermilion red and a gold-yellow, – set off by a quiet cold tone of green and by a pearly white, go to make up a superb symphony, evoking a richness of autumn and the splendid luxuriance of the fields. Thus we have a still-life with a commonplace subject arousing in us awareness of the beauty of the world and the benign sweetness of life. For Bonnard, although his art deliberately re-creates reality, yet succeeds in identifying himself with these natural forces. He is thus at the opposite pole from the Impressionists: they are concerned with reproducing Nature, while he interprets it – as boldly as a Matisse or a Picasso. What is most remarkable is that this same boldness is not in the least apparent, so well does it go along with the ease of execution and seeming spontaneity. 'To conceal art by art' – that old dream of Chardin and indeed of the whole French tradition in art – no one has ever brought it off better than Bonnard, who has here even allowed himself to heighten the natural image with a kind of playful mischief and an often ironic fantasy.

Shown at the Salon des Indépendants, 1936 (No. 425). Purchased by the State, 1936. Musée du Luxembourg.

PIERRE BONNARD (1867–1947) 1938–45, signed
ENTRANCE TO THE HARBOUR OF TROUVILLE Oil on wood
Height 77 cm. (30¹/₄″)
Width 103 cm. (40¹/₂″)
This painting shows how far Bonnard differed from the Impressionists.
They preferred to work straight from their subject; Bonnard finished at
Le Cannet in 1945 this canvas begun seven years earlier at Trouville.
Wary of 'opening a window on Nature', he always made his composition
with great care; and although colour is used here to express light, it is
used quite differently, less precisely but more poetically – when, indeed,
were these golden greys ever seen in Normandy? That he rejects the Impressionist aim of realism is also shown by the absence of an horizon. But his
lyricism never slides into the sort of pantheistic medley to which Monet
succumbed towards the end of his life. The former Nabi tempers his
fervent outpourings with a sly wit. Bought from the artist by the Musées
his life. Purchased from the artist by the Musées Nationaux, 1946.

PIERRE BONNARD (1867–1947)
Mediterranean

1941–44, signed
Gouache on paper
Height 50 cm. (19¹/₂″)
Width 63 cm. (24³/₄″)

After settling in Le Cannet about 1910, Bonnard made many paintings of the region, working with an imaginative freedom that can be appreciated in this fine gouache. He is here not really concerned to reproduce the setting of Cannes with its bay and the Estérel beyond, or with rendering the light of the Côte d'Azur and the waters of the Mediterranean. He is taken up with composing a symphony in blues. He sets off these various blues in their sombre harmony by tones of white and black, as well as by accents of red ochre arranged in parallel bands. This gives the work a grave splendour which expresses the mood of Bonnard during the last years of his life.

Purchased from the artist by the Musées Nationaux, 1946.

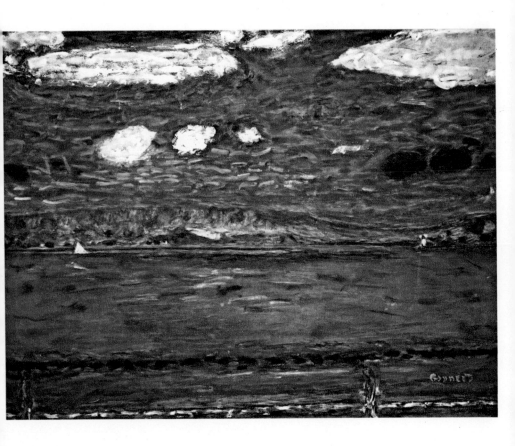

FELIX VALLOTTON (1865–1925)
GALLERY AT THE THÉÂTRE DU CHÂTELET

1895, signed and dated
Oil on board
Height 50 cm. (19¹/₂″)
Width 62 cm. (24¹/₂″)

Bonnard, Vuillard and Vallotton are the true contemporaries of Jules Renard and the *Revue Blanche*. What irony there is in this picture, where the almost caricatured bearing of the individuals goes so well with the drollness of the composition! These qualities of observation, wittily cynical, should not obscure those belonging strictly to painting. Vallotton deliberately limits his colour to a minor key, giving it subtleties, amusing dissonances and audacity, enhanced by the certainty of touch and the shimmer of the paint. The art of summarizing and implication are here brought to a climax. The ingenuity of the composition, intentionally out of centre and balance, combines with the freshness of his angle of vision to achieve a decorative quality, dignity of style, and wit. Carle Dreyfus Bequest, 1953.

FELIX VALLOTTON (1865–1925)   1899, signed and dated
LE DÎNER, EFFET DE LAMPE   Oil on wood
                                              Height 57 cm. (22¹/₂″)
                                               Width 89 cm. (35″)

How much the Nabis owe to Japanese art is proved by this painting, no
less than by Bonnard's *The Peignoir* (see page 78). Here, however, the
model is not the *kakemonos* but the colour prints of the Ukiyo-e, with their
flat tints, their silhouettes like those of the shadow-play, and their compositions that we relish for their unexpectedness. What Vallotton adds to
these is first the curiosity about the effects of artificial light that he shares
with Toulouse-Lautrec, Bonnard and Vuillard, who, like himself, led the reaction against Impressionism with its passion for sunlight. Secondly, he shows
a kind of sarcastic humour which has even more point when we realise that
the figures portrayed are himself (back view), his wife (extreme right) and
his step-children, whose likeness he has caught even to their mannerisms.
He shows one of his stepsons gnawing away at a crust of bread, as he loved
to do.

   In face of this rather merciless, homely tone and the almost carica-
tural style, we come to understand why the German Expressionists, in

SUZANNE VALADON (1867–1938) 1909, signed and dated
ADAM AND EVE Oil on canvas
Height 162 cm. (63³/₄")
Width 131 cm. (51¹/₂")

Marie Clémentine, known as Suzanne Valadon, was not only a most forceful feminine personality, but also an essentially independent artist. Her
early work impressed Toulouse-Lautrec, and Degas gave her immense
encouragement; she herself admired Gauguin and Cézanne. These influences
she melted down in the crucible of a powerful temperament, setting her
own stamp upon them. There are good grounds for claiming her as a
representative of early Expressionism, which appeared in Paris alongside
Fauvism from 1900 to 1910 or thereabouts, when it was also taking hold
in Germany. The vigorous drawing she derives from Degas, the skill in
portraying character by a few summary and incisive strokes from Lautrec;
from Cézanne she learnt to convey plasticity by colour, from Gauguin the
use of a rich yet muted chromatism, a shimmering paint and decorative
experiment. But the originality of Suzanne Valadon is unqualified in these
nudes, portraits of herself and her young husband André Utter (born 1886)
whom she had just married in 1909. The uncompromising naturalism of
the figures and the way she brings out the character of each with powerful
feeling and sensuality, the almost caricatured look she gives to her own
face, the authority in uniting the fruits of reflection and spontaneity, the
ease with which she blends incongruous elements and her paradoxical
experiments – all these are peculiarly her own – like the deliberately coarse
accent by which she arrives at a robust poetry, one that has a tang of the
people without losing its rare distinction.
The painting was purchased by the State from the artist.

Continued from page 89

particular the painters of *Die Brücke*, should so often have drawn on Vallotton. With Toulouse-Lautrec, Matisse, Van Gogh and Munch, he provided
the sources of their painting and wood engraving. Purchased by the
Musées Nationaux in 1947.

MAURICE UTRILLO (1883–1955) c. 1909, signed
THE GARDEN AT MONTMAGNY Oil on cardboard
Height 52 cm. (20¹/₂″)
Width 75 cm. (29¹/₂″)

Utrillo was induced to paint by his mother, Suzanne Valadon, who hoped to rescue him from his chronic drunkenness. A painter in spite of himself, almost from the start he accomplished masterpieces such as this picture. The manner in which he draws these trees and the leaden, gloomy light recall his earlier paintings at Montmagny, but the predominant white of the house and the garden wall heralds his 'White period'. The tension of line, subtle shading and harmony of tones, the power expressed in the form, the breadth of handling – all make this one of Utrillo's most successful canvases. From the sodden atmosphere and harsh cold of this garden, the peeling walls, the desolateness of the gloomy house and the absence of any human creature is drawn a bitter and appealing poetry. Utrillo Exhibition, Galerie Renou et Colle, 1936. Purchased by the State, 1936.

92

MAURICE UTRILLO (1883–1955)   1910, signed
VIEW OF MONTMARTRE   Oil on canvas
Height 73 cm. (28³/₄″)
Width 102 cm. (40¹/₈″)

After Montmagny and the northern outskirts of Paris, Utrillo's choice of
territory, especially from 1910 to 1914, was the Butte Montmartre. Here
he painted some of the outstanding works of his 'White period', with an
art that gradually became less harsh. His palette increased in nuance and
range; subtle pinks appear beside whites which grow creamier. The skies
become loftier and thin-spun and a more pearly light spreads a delicate
chequering over walls and houses. Nevertheless the form does not lose
definition, for Utrillo puts this light into the pigment itself. This rich, thick
pigment, to which he might add sand or plaster to get closer to the nature
of his subject, serves to express both volume and atmosphere, and at the
same time, through its perfection as a medium and its poetic import, gives
the work its plastic beauty and human emotive power. Lent by the Commission de Récupération Artistique, 1950.

GEORGES ROUAULT (1871–1958)   1906, signed
Au Miroir   Watercolour on cardboard
                                            Height 70 cm. (27$^{1}/_{2}$")
                                            Width 53 cm. (21")

Rouault, working on the theme of the prostitute in the wake of Degas and
Toulouse-Lautrec, does this in a spirit and with an art entirely different
from theirs. First, he expands the theme of these girls into some general and
universal concept – a theme to which those other painters like to give a
flavour of 'the modern'. No defined setting here; no accessory detail; the
nude, universal and not set in time, takes the place of the garment, that
particularises. The portrait of an individual yields place to the type. Stress
on the 'thing seen' gives way to a visionary's rich imagination. Instead of
the scornful irony of Degas or the sardonic smile of Toulouse-Lautrec,
Rouault, the Christian, feels indignation and pain; yet he does not pass
judgment, but subdues his anger with an infinite compassion. Not that this
pity leads him to gloss over his repugnance for these girls or the ignominy
they have come to. They have never been portrayed more authentically or
with such mastery – a mastery that makes Rouault a forerunner of the
Expressionists, and an unequalled one. Broad, powerful and definitive in
concept, the outline drawing poses the figure of the girl and fixes the
character. The form has a superb self-possession – the modelling being
achieved by the colour rather than by chiaroscuro – and this quality of
dignity serves to divest the figure of any vulgarity and to raise it on to
an impressive plane. The colour also provides the contrasts: to the vigour
of the blues and blacks is added the delicacy of the pinks. The execution,
too, is astonishing in its authority and spontaneity. Rouault had a great
liking for water-colour at this time, not solely for its effect of transparency
but also because its swift handling made it the best medium for the flash
and quiver of his sensitivity. We have to go back to Daumier and Goya
to find anything comparable to this blend of power and mastery, of horror
and the sublime, of supreme artistry and vibrant humanity.

Shown at the Salon des Indépendants, 1906 (Catalogue No. 4539). Private
collection, Lyons. Purchased by the Musées Nationaux, 1951.

GEORGES ROUAULT (1871–1958)
THE APPRENTICE

c. 1925
Oil on canvas
Height 68 cm. (26³/₄″)
Width 52 cm. (20¹/₂″)

From 1918 to 1930, Rouault turned inward for his inspiration, gaining in concentration what he lost in fierce vehemence, and his craft became more and more taken up with technical problems of painting as such. It may be that his work on ceramics which occupied him from 1907 to 1914, and on engraving to which he devoted his best efforts from 1917 to 1925, have some bearing on the new interests that absorbed Rouault. In any case it is significant that from 1910, and even more from 1920 onwards, he developed a constant preference for painting in oils. The spontaneous handling required for a water-colour is superseded by the intellectual process of reflection necessary in the slower medium. Certainly, the blues that continue to dominate in Rouault's chromatism are a proof of the consistency of his genius and so are his attachment to chiaroscuro and to the outlines that determine the form. These blues come to have a new depth, extremely rich and enigmatic, and the outlines point to fresh experiments in rhythm and harmony. In this picture it will be seen how the drawing of the rim of the hat follows the line of the forehead and exaggerates it, while the line of the chin runs counter to it; also that Rouault has deliberately contrasted the vertical lines of the neck, the horizontal lines of the shirt-front, and the segmented curves of the shoulders. This is not to say, however, that he falls into the decorative. The quietness of these simple lines holds the seeds of the same tension as the criss-cross tangle of hectic strokes he liked to make in his earlier years, and the quietness calls forth forms even wider in concept in their new hieratic style. Furthermore, the works of Rouault take on such a depth reflected from his inner life that often, in looking at them, Rembrandt comes to mind. This self-portrait, entitled by Rouault *The Apprentice* with his usual humility, bears comparison with the self-portraits of Rembrandt that most reflect his spiritual nature.

Remained in the artist's possession until 1952. Shown in the Rouault Exhibition at the Musée National d'Art Moderne, Paris, 1952 (No. 43). Presented anonymously, 1952.

GEORGES ROUAULT (1871–1958)
THE HOLY FACE

1933, signed
Oil on canvas
Height 91 cm. (36″)
Width 65 cm. (25¹/₂″)

Rouault was a Christian of deep conviction and after 1914 often painted religious pictures, inspired especially by the mystery of the Passion. He reacted violently (and fortunately) against absurd precepts governing religious art from the time of Guido Reni, Murillo and Mignard. In that reaction he rediscovered the sense of the Passion so faithfully portrayed by the Masters of the fifteenth century (in particular *Christ on the Cross,* the altarpiece at Isenheim by Mathias Grünewald, and the *Christ in prayer* in the Cathedral of Perpignan). Moreover, he succeeds in giving the bloodstreaked, ravaged face of the Man of Sorrows the sublime nobility of God in Majesty as we see it in Romanesque and Byzantine art. This particular picture has a grandeur and holiness that derive from the artist's return to the sources of the great Christian tradition. Equally, it has a fineness of workmanship that is clearly perceptible in his handling of the paint. Rouault had been convinced by Gustave Moreau of the soundness of his axiom that a painting possesses an 'indispensable richness', and so he sets out to give the pigment on his brush the intrinsic beauty possessed by the equivalent materials used in ceramics, enamels and stained glass. By tireless effort he succeeds in transmuting the paste squeezed from a tube into a substance of depth and splendour, through which the light filters and colours glow iridescent – all with a rare and masterly technique.

Presented by Mrs Chester Dale, 1933, Musée du Luxembourg.

GEORGES ROUAULT (1871–1958)   1939–45, signed
Homo homini lupus   Oil on paper mounted on linen
                                          Height 64 cm. (25¼")
                                           Width 46 cm. (18")

Rouault, in the calm of old age and soothed by the practice of his art, and
more and more absorbed by the beauty of the paint itself, only on rare
occasions found inspiration in the Second World War. The First World War,
on the contrary, had moved him to paint the whole of the second part of
his *Miserere* (originally *War* and *Miserere*). This picture, called by him
Homo homini lupus, is his only comment on the tragic conflict of 1939–45
and the horrors of the Occupation. But it is made with unrivalled power.
How one is gripped by his symbolic summary of the tragedy of those
events–by this hanged and broken man, harrowing as those of Villon's
ballad ; the house going up in flames and the blood-red moon ! The drawing
has extraordinary power, vast in concept and harsh, making the broken
segments outlining the body of the hanged man stand out against the long
lines of the gallows and the disk of the moon. Nor is contrast lacking–
the gleam of this ghastly white of the shirt with the fiery and muted tones
that dominate the canvas. The chiaroscuro, too, makes the drama of the
scene echo with all its tragic significance. Lastly, the thickness of the
pigment, opaque as enamel, intensifies the vibration of the colour and the
light. These features taken together reflect exactly Rouault's sense of horror
and make this work a most devastating allegory of the monstrous evils of
modern warfare, and in this it can stand beside Picasso's *Guernica.*

But, while Picasso's picture breathes only rage and despair, in this
canvas of Rouault, the Christian, notes of peace and of hope are sounded.
The dead man seems to make a motion of resignation with his open hands,
and even more significantly, in the upper left of the canvas, high, beyond
the gallows, above the moon, shines a pale star–a star that appears here as
in the last line of Dante's *Inferno* and seems to bear the same meaning : it
is certainly a message of love and redemption that it brings to us by its
humble triumph over the power of darkness.

Presented by the artist in 1949.

GEORGES ROUAULT (1871–1958)   1952
Christian Nocturne   Oil on canvas
                                                  Height 97 cm. (38″)
                                                  Width 52 cm. (20¹/₂″)

This is one of the outstanding works of Rouault's old age. It is a remarkable fact that at eighty years of age the artist was able to find a renewal of his powers and to adopt a new manner. There is no doubt that the extreme thickness of the pigment, literally piled up to give an appearance of being done in relief, is but the final stage in a development that began in 1910, leading him after 1935 to lay layer upon layer of colour. The palette, however, was radically modified in his last paintings. In place of the dominant blues accompanied here and there by reds, yellows and greens of a metallic richness predominate. As often happens with painters in their old age (we have only to think of the Cézanne of 1900, for instance), Rouault in his eighties returned to his youth. Going back beyond his tranquil years 1935 to 1950, and the religious stresses of the 1914 to 1935 period, he recaptured the dynamic force that was implicit in his work from 1905 to 1914. Here curves predominate once more and introduce into the composition a sense of movement disdained by the artist for more than thirty years. Even the horizon is a curve which increases the curvature of the islands and at the same time takes the eye up to the curve of the clouds, and the moon above. The whole pulse and rhythm of the cosmos seem to throb through this landscape. All the same, though we may sense behind this painting a long line of landscapes equally imaginary and equally peopled by sacred figures, here a new feeling informs the images. Certainly the religious note was already apparent from 1930 onwards in a number of other 'Christian landscapes' or 'Biblical landscapes', where Rouault touches a religious grandeur without any recourse to traditional conventions; no halos or customary attributes express the holiness of the figures, but their religious character was none-the-less so clear that anyone could recognize – as in this canvas – Christ, the Virgin, the Apostles and the Holy Women.

Not until now, however, had Rouault's spirituality been expressed in this style of rapturous and jubilant fervour. Hitherto, it had been by turns sorrowful, grave, equable; now it made this discovery of joy. And joy, in tune with the illimitable life of the universe, here breaks out with an exulting force. It is a paean to divine majesty and goodness, as it were his 'Ninth Symphony', where man, who has passed out of anger into joyous triumph, achieves his evolution and, by way of Purgatory and Hell, ascends to Paradise. Purchased from the artist by the Musées Nationaux, 1952.

HENRI MATISSE (1869–1954)   1907, signed
Le Luxe, I   Oil on canvas
Height 210 cm. (82$^{1}/_{2}$″)
Width 138 cm. (54$^{1}/_{2}$″)

This is the first version of a painting which in its final form hangs in the Copenhagen Art Gallery. It was painted in 1907 in the Catalan port of Collioure, and this landscape gave Matisse his background. It is a clear example of his Fauve manner. Fauvism is not for him the elation of a palette of intoxicating colour, as it is for Vlaminck or Derain; rather, it entails the reduction of painting to a few resources, colours and arabesques in particular, that suffice to express all. Thus we find in this canvas that space, form and light are created by contrasting zones of colour. Henceforth Matisse is able to dispense with chiaroscuro, gradations of tone, 'passages' or transitions, values, modelling and perspective; by this means he gets a unity of surface as well as a decorative and, as it were, architectural quality. Here he re-discovers the spirit and even the processes of the Romanesque fresco. We can observe how, in order to give a certain illusion of space and light, he spreads bands differing in tone behind his figures. The Romanesque painters, however, were less concerned with representation, while Matisse gives these bands a guise of realism, suggesting beach, sea, mountain and skies.

In the Salon d'Automne 1907 (Catalogue No. 758). Purchased from the artist by the Musées Nationaux, 1945.

HENRI MATISSE (1869–1954)   1916
THE PAINTER AND HIS MODEL   Oil on canvas

Height 147 cm. (58″)

Width 97 cm. (38″)

Matisse was the leading spirit in the Fauve movement. Even so, between 1913 and 1917 he yielded in a tentative way to the influence of Cubism, as can be detected in this canvas, painted in his studio on the Quai Saint Michel. Here again we find the same view from the window as in his *Interior with Goldfish* of 1914, his *Studio* of 1916, and others. It has been very much worked over and had matured chiefly from the *Girl in green dress* (1916). The inclination of Matisse at that time towards a severe art is seen in his muted and quiet chromatism with a basis of blacks and greys; in simplified forms expressed in a geometric manner; in the rejection of sinuous arabesques in favour of segments of rectilinears and obliques; and also a still greater preciseness in dividing up and sharply contrasting the colour zones. But the presence of a baroque mirror (a feature that is seen again in the *Decorative figure on an ornamental background* of 1927) reveals how far Matisse has in fact got away from Cubism and how near he is to abandoning this severe manner, which is thought to be one of his best.

The painting was in the Salon des Indépendants in 1926. Salon d'Automne, 1945, (No. XI). Purchased from the artist by the Musées Nationaux, 1945.

HENRI MATISSE (1869–1954)
THE BUFFET

1928, signed and dated
Oil on canvas
Height 83 cm. (32¹/₂″)
Width 103 cm. (40¹/₂″)

After a period of rather facile work, roughly between 1918 and 1927, Matisse returned to a more disciplined art. He created a kind of synthesis between the sumptuous colour of his Fauve period and the severe construction of his quasi-Cubist phase, turning to Cézanne as a model, as before in 1900–01. His subject, the dominant blue, the accentuated structure of the shapes and of the picture as a whole, the indication of depth by diagonals such as the door ajar and the knife laid crosswise – all show this turning back to Cézanne, even though he kept to his own very personal taste for economy of paint and austerity in handling. Presented by the Association des Amis des Artistes Vivants, 1929.

HENRI MATISSE (1869–1954)
Red still-life with Magnolia

1941, signed and dated
Oil on canvas
Height 73 cm. (28³/₄")
Width 100 cm. (39¹/₂")

Matisse, in a film dealing with him, spoke of his affection for this still-life. This preference is easily understood. The picture succeeds as a work of very high quality, and its individual character is typical of Matisse: the flexible and simple, austere drawing, the brilliant colour, and the areas of white canvas left unpainted which, with the adjacent colours, express superbly the pearly whiteness of the flower. But the most striking feature of the work is its composition, achieved by juxtaposing objects balanced with such perfect mastery that the arrangement could not be disturbed without spoiling its harmony. The mass of vase and flower fills the middle of the canvas from top to bottom; it is flanked by four unrelated components placed to the extreme right and left. Matisse may have been unaware in making this scheme that he was returning to a type of composition favoured

HENRI MATISSE (1869–1954)
Roumanian blouse

1940, signed and dated
Oil on canvas
Height 92 cm. (36¼")
Width 73 cm. (28¾")

How this picture came to be painted we know from a film on Matisse made in 1945 by the Compagnie Générale Cinématographique. Ten versions, it seems, were made between December 1939 and May 1940, and in the film we can watch step by step the labour of discarding and composing afresh by the artist under the spell of the beauty of a blouse – the same that inspired another canvas of that period, the *Sleeping Woman*. Matisse began with a work which kept close to the visible facts, admittedly commonplace; then he proceeded to eliminate detail, to summarise the main features and to create a stylised image of the subject, finally arriving at this canvas, where bare indication of the two motifs of the embroidery suggests the lavish gaudy colours of the garment more surely than would a faithful delineation, and where, too, the distortion of face and figure brings out the underlying character. Thus we become very aware of the personality of the artist, whose genius, like that of Degas, is less in the nature of an inborn talent than the fruit of intelligence and reflection, of his method and his will.

Salon d'Automne, 1945 (No. XVIII). Presented by the artist, 1953.

Continued from page 109

in Romanesque art, and especially used in the Catalan antependia, where the person of Christ fills the whole upper space of the central area and the symbols of the four Evangelists balance it to right and left in two pairs, in the upper and lower corners. Thus the relation between the two types of composition is close, and a feature of modern painting is illuminated by it: we can see its kinship with the paintings of the Middle Ages, for both are founded on a common quest for decorative effect.

Purchased from the artist by the Musées Nationaux, 1945.

HENRI MATISSE (1869–1954) Large Interior in Red

1948, signed and dated
Oil on canvas
Height 146 cm. (57$^{1}/_{2}$")
Width 57 cm. (22$^{1}/_{2}$")

This canvas represents, very freely, the artist's studio at Vence, and it is a synthesis as well as the climax of the paintings Matisse did from 1946 to 1948. Two of these works *(The Pineapple* and *Intérieur à la fenêtre au palmier)* have a place in the background in this picture, and those same plants, flowers, fruit and furniture that the artist liked at this time to introduce in his compositions are seen again. Here, too, Matisse applies the principles of grouping seen in the *Red Still-life with magnolia,* only here he uses them with much greater boldness. There is no longer a central motif. Instead there are four, one in each corner – the square table, the round table, the picture and the sketch. Although they all vary in shape and size, there is counterpoise because the colours, in greater contrast on the left than on the right, redeem this inequality. The unity of the painting does not on that account fall short of perfection: not only does the arm-chair weld together the four parts of the grouping but the over-all 'tonal' colour has the effect of securing the total cohesion of the work. The whole is suffused by a harmony of reds which gives the impression of light, of coolness and fragrance, of that sensuous calm that Matisse has many times expressed in his paintings. Did he not remark somewhere about 1907, 'I should like any man who is feeling defeated to gain a sense of calm and repose when he looks at my paintings.' One day, however, he told me that by this repose he meant that kind of tonic renewal of the whole physical well-being felt after a spell of winter sports. This picture is wholly taut, nervous and masculine, for Matisse takes his means, of drawing, colour and form, to the highest point of intensity and then demands of them a super-lative efficiency. Perhaps it is because he 'simplified painting', as his master Gustave Moreau prophesied he would, that Matisse has so important a place in the history of art.

Matisse Exhibition, Musée National d'Art Moderne, 1949 (Catalogue No. 13). Purchased from the artist by the State.

ALBERT MARQUET (1875–1947) 1904, signed and dated
PORTRAIT OF ANDRÉ ROUVEYRE Oil on canvas
Height 92 cm. (36¹/₄")
Width 61 cm. (24")

Marquet, with his friend Matisse, was from 1898 one of the early followers of the Fauves. Fortunately, however, he never allowed himself to be imprisoned in the cage of any school – not even during his Fauve years. Some of his paintings of that time are typically Fauve in the way they exalt colour and fantasy in tone (for example, *The beach at Fécamp* of 1906, page 117). But many others can only be associated rather remotely with the art of the group, and we have an example in this portrait of André Rouveyre, writer, critic and graphic artist, who was a close friend of Matisse and Marquet. The Musée d'Art Moderne possesses a portrait of him drawn by Matisse.

Here, Marquet is not seeing with the eyes of the Neo-Impressionists, or of Cézanne or Gauguin – as Matisse was doing at this time – and he is unaffected by Van Gogh, whose art had intoxicated Vlaminck. Rather, like Van Dongen, he goes to Manet as a master, whose refusal of restraints in his craft and simplifying audacity of vision appeal to him. In the manner of *The Fife Player*, Marquet dispenses with background, and by his extraordinarily decided brushwork conjures up the figure of his sitter, a black mass modelled by the brush-strokes alone: note especially how the direction of the brush-work suggests where the jacket is undone. Fauvism for Marquet (as often for Matisse) is not so much a partiality for intense colour as for synthesis and summarizing, when painting is reduced to the arabesque, to tone and to brush-work. This portrait is astonishing in its veiled temerity, and in this respect it outstrips what was being done in Germany at that time – what Munch, and later the disciples of *Die Brücke*, were to achieve in a similar spirit of bold venture.

Purchased from M. André Rouveyre by the Musées Nationaux in 1939.

ALBERT MARQUET (1875–1947)
THE PONT NEUF AT NIGHT

1935–39, signed
Oil on canvas
Height 81 cm. (32")
Width 100 cm. (39¹/₂")

This painting is a *tour de force* on the part of Marquet, an artist who was usually so judicious in the way he put his means to work. Most striking is the bold manner in which he distributes the accents of colour and gets a balanced composition. The hot tones form a diagonal band, while high up on the right there is a startling cold blue that has no complement on the left: even so, the composition is not thrown out of symmetry. It is balanced in effect by some acid yellows on the lower left hand, which thus bring off the harmony and cohesion of the whole. Presented by the artist in 1940.

ALBERT MARQUET (1875–1947)
The beach at Fécamp

1906, signed
Oil on canvas
Height 51 cm. (20″)
Width 61 cm. (24″)

Marquet is a Fauve of a rather special kind, as this picture demonstrates. Clearly he is not afraid of bold colours, and with the utmost frankness and blatancy he sets the green of the cliff beside the blue of the sailors' jerseys and the red of the flag. But his Fauvism lies much more in the elliptical and expressive strength of the calligraphy. One or two brush-strokes apparently tossed off, and there we have a whole crowd of bathers in movement at the water's edge, conjured up decisively and with verve. This art of expressing much in a few strokes is seen again in Marquet's way of suggesting space without using perspective, simply by the accuracy of the summary relations he sets up between simplified planes – the relation of

CHARLES CAMOIN (born 1879) 1904, signed
PORTRAIT OF ALBERT MARQUET Oil on canvas
Height 92 cm. (36¹/₄")
Width 73 cm. (28³/₄")

Camoin met Matisse and Marquet (as he did Manguin) at the Ecole des Beaux Arts in the studio of Gustave Moreau, a nursery of Fauvism. His fellow-students drew him to this style, and for a time he painted in a way so closely in tune with theirs that this picture was long thought to be a self-portrait by Marquet. Not until Camoin happened to see and recognise the canvas was it ascribed to him. It is evidence of the friendship of Camoin and Marquet and the close relation, at the time, of their art, as well as a wholly successful achievement in technique and imagination. There is the authoritative draughtsmanship, elliptical and powerfully allusive, the bold choice of colour that has a monochrome harmony and yet shades of variation, the art of expressing the form without modelling or values, by outlines marking it off from the background and bounding its various elements. All these factors give the portrait a lively, sparkling assurance and a good-natured and amused irony. Presented by Mme Albert Marquet in 1948.

Continued from page 117

light included. Can we speak of Impressionism in this connection? Hardly, because although his attempt to render light relates him to Monet, Marquet's method of expressing it emphasizes his distance from the Impressionists. He does not so much analyse light as re-create it by a kind of rippling of tones as in watered silk. Note the originality of the means he uses to put the sea into the light and make a play of light on it. This produces a subtlety of tones which was to go on developing and, from 1909 onwards, to lead him towards greys, in which he excelled. But for all that he did not turn his back on Fauvism; the simplifying synthesis, the summarised style of his drawing and of his planes, and his aim at unity and cohesion were to bind Marquet for a long time, if not for the rest of his life, to the art of his youth.

Bequest of M. Paul Jamot, 1940.

KEES VAN DONGEN (born 1877)
DANCER

c. 1907, signed
Oil on canvas
Height 115 cm. (45^1/$_4$″)
Width 75 cm. (29^1/$_2$″)

This work belongs to Van Dongen's Fauve period, a time when he was displaying to the full his rich and far-ranging talents. Certainly the bold statement and the brilliance of the colour relate the particular style he uses here to Fauvism. The main links with it, however, are the simplified drawing of the contour, the decisiveness of the brush-work, the broad handling and the cutting out of detail and accessories. Another link is provided by the omission of 'passages' or transitions and of light and shade; also by the synthesis, spontaneous and wilful, and in the dashing and masterly way he confines himself in his work to the use of a few essential means, such as the arabesque, tone and impasto. Van Dongen has something in common with Manet, if we judge by some of these features: there is his mastery of the brush-work as well as the precision and authority of the handling. On the other hand, in place of the aristocratic manner and subtlety of Manet, he gives a sturdy zest to his work and an accent that is deliberately coarse – even provocatively vulgar. Nevertheless, this style often endows painting – as it does here – with an authentic poetic quality.

Presented by the Association des Amis des Artistes Vivantes, 1929.

RAOUL DUFY (1877–1953)
Posters at Trouville

1906, signed
Oil on canvas
Height 65 cm. (25$^{1}/_{2}$″)
Width 81 cm. (32″)

Raoul Dufy was born at Le Havre, which may perhaps account for his Impressionist vision and sensibility, influenced in due course by the Fauvism he took up towards 1903. He was an intimate of Marquet, and in the summer of 1906 the friends spent some days at Trouville in painting the same subject, one that so enchanted Dufy that he made two versions of it. This canvas is startling in colour and also gains much from the nimble and witty drawing, the swift brush-stroke and the oddities of the lay-out. Already Dufy proves himself a superb draughtsman as with off-hand mastery he puts in the figure in the panama – the playwright Henri Bernstein.
Salon d'Automne, 1906 (No. 512). Bought by the Musées Nationaux, 1956.

RAOUL DUFY (1877–1953)
THE PADDOCK AT DEAUVILLE

c. 1930, signed
Oil on canvas
Height 54 cm. (21¹/₄″)
Width 130 cm. (51″)

Dufy was enthralled by movement in modern life and diverted by its spectacle, which he regarded with an ironic eye. He painted race meetings many times, thus providing the succession to Degas. Here, however, he has wished less to paint horses, jockeys, the race crowd – entirely omitted from this picture – than to give his impression of a lovely summer's day, with all its sunlight and warmth. He has conceived his picture as a harmony in red and blue.

In the middle and a little towards the left, there is a great splash of red which is taken up on the sides by a series of lesser notes. On the left this *decrescendo* is a paling of colour that goes from red to pink, while to the right a darkening of tone takes the red to brown. Above is a great band of azure blue, and below, a series of little blue dabs that are so many rhyming notes of colour. Nothing is left to chance in this composition, which has all the artistry of a fugue: nor is the off-hand, careless, childish look unstudied. 'Art to conceal art', the remark of Chardin (echoing Racine: '*faire difficilement des vers faciles*') Dufy could adopt as his own.

Presented by the Association des Amis des Artistes Vivants, 1932.

123

RAOUL DUFY (1877–1953) 1931
RIDERS UNDER THE TREES Oil on canvas
Height 213 cm. (84″)
Width 262 cm. (103″)

Raoul Dufy was commissioned in 1930 by an Englishman, J. B. A. Kessler, to paint his portrait and that of his wife and five daughters, all on horse-back. After spending several months in England making sketches for the work, he painted this canvas during the autumn of 1931. But the work remained in his studio, since the British Customs made so much difficulty about allowing it into England that the artist judged it simpler to go over to London in 1932 to paint a second version on the spot – the version which he gave to Mr Kessler and which is still in the possession of his heirs. Although the subject bristled with problems for him, Dufy nevertheless achieved one of his finest works. There is a superlative ease in composition, the drawing is deft and sure, the colour brilliant. Above all, faithful portrai-ture, a mural quality and a sense of poetry are perfectly blended. By rendering line and colour independently, as always, Dufy sets his figures in the light and atmosphere, gives an impression of the wind swaying the leaves, shifts light and shadow on his shapes and constantly modifies their tones and contours. But, he does not confine this method to the surrounding air, like the Impressionists; the independence of line and colour gives a decorative effect such as is created in the same way in fifteenth-century tapestries. Dufy also achieves this decorative quality by purposely not hollowing his canvas, by hanging behind his figures a curtain of trees against which they stand out, by enlivening his dead zones with such details as the butterfly and bees of the foreground. Nor is this effect achieved at the expense of an element of poetry. The ingenuity of his colour, the lightness of his shapes, the vibrancy of his brushwork – all enable him to create about this group of middle-class English people on horseback an air of immateriality, of fantasy even, so that they become the descendants of *seigneurs* portrayed by the Limbourg brothers in the fairy-tale cavalcades of the *Très Riches Heures* of the Duc de Berry.

Retrospective Raoul Dufy Exhibition at Musée National d'Art Moderne, 1953 (No. 75). Presented by the artist's widow, 1954.

LOUIS VALTAT (1869–1952)
THE MERRY-GO-ROUND

1895–96, signed
Oil on canvas
Height 46 cm. (18″)
Width 55 cm. (21¹/₂″)

Valtat is one of those minor artists whose work has great zest and flavour. With his amused and compassionate sense of contemporary life he stood close to the Nabis, but his work was related to the Fauves by the conciseness of his drawing and his form and the expressive style of his brushwork. The tones favoured by the Nabis and the vivid colours of the Fauves marry happily; the poetry lies half-way between the compassionate irony of Bonnard and Vuillard and the sardonically objective vision of the Fauves, Marquet and Dufy. Purchased by the Musées Nationaux in 1951.

MAURICE DE VLAMINCK (1876–1958)
LANDSCAPE WITH RED TREES

1906, signed
Oil on canvas
Height 65 cm. (25¹/₂″)
Width 81 cm. (32″)

As early as 1898, Matisse and Marquet were propagating the ideas of Fauvism, of which Vlaminck is held to be the most typical exponent. In 1902 he became the founder and a member with Derain of the so-called 'Ecole de Chatou', and the painting of these red trees illustrates perfectly the aesthetic and ethics of the Fauves. 'Art', Vlaminck wrote, 'is as individual as love,' and Fauve painting in its exalting of the individual interprets what is personal to each of us, namely sensation. However, simple sensation does not allow us to know lines or shapes or space, creations of the abstractive faculties of the intellect or fruits of the association of ideas, but solely colours. Therefore we find Vlaminck reducing his drawing to a

MAURICE DE VLAMINCK (1876–1958)   1920, signed
THE HOUSE WITH LEAN-TO   Oil on canvas
                                                   Height 90 cm. (35¹/₂″)
                                                   Width 70 cm. (27¹/₂″)

Vlaminck, more than any other Fauve, put pure colour before all else, but later he turned his interest to the compositional structure. This picture is an example of his Cézanne style; the subject itself is reminiscent of Cézanne's *Farm at Bellevue*. The execution is one of exalted mood. The relation of the blues to the dark greens and, in their midst, the house standing out stark and livid, with a look of wretchedness given by the gaping windows, the lowering clouds, the neglected garden, the movement that shivers through all shapes, even to the posts and the roof of the lean-to – all are features that recur from the start to finish of Vlaminck's career and make him the most expressionist of the Fauves. Purchased by the State in 1925.

Continued from page 127

kind of shorthand and flattening the values which occur in a flat world. His absorbing interest is in colour, which he develops to its greatest intensity as he applies it straight from the tube, without breaking it up or modifying it, while at the same time sharpening the tones by contrasts. This colour, then, is subjective. He does not paint objects in their real colour but as he sees them, systematically heightening his sensation of colour the better to communicate it to us: the russet bark of the trees here becomes vermilion. This subjectivity shows itself even in the execution. Every brush-stroke can be seen, so that the paint carries in its very substance the stamp of the hand that laid it on, and reveals the creative emotion and impulse of the artist. No other Fauve carried this subjectivism, sensualism and chromatic ecstasy further than Vlaminck between the years 1902 and 1908. It is clear that he had absorbed from the works of Van Gogh, which caused such a stir at the Galerie Bernheim exhibition in 1901, their full implications, and he has achieved in this canvas a work of splendid force and momentum.

In the Le Guillou sale, 1946, at Nantes (No. 7). Purchased by the Musées Nationaux.

ANDRÉ DERAIN (1880–1954)   1905, signed
THE OLD TREE   Oil on canvas
                                                         Height 41 cm. (16")
                                                          Width 33 cm. (13")

Derain was closely associated with Vlaminck, whom he met by chance at
Chatou and with whom he worked side by side from about 1902 to 1907.
He nevertheless differed widely from him in nature and outlook, which
explains the resemblances and the differences in the Fauve works of the
two painters. Both men have a love for intensity of tones that can express
in the aggregate the colour of the objects, the light that falls on them, the
space containing them and the actual paint. Both have a preference for
broad, generous, decided handling, interpreting the impulse of the heart
and the bidding of instinct. In both, Fauvism stands for revolutionary
boldness and is vehement, intoxicated and expressionist, with the urge to
do something new, in defiance of taboos. Derain, however, cultivated where
his friend was rough, reflective where he was impulsive, felt always more
constrained to hold his work in check and to paint in less headlong fashion.
The colour in most of his Fauve works is, as here, less blatant than
Vlaminck's. Instead of strident flourishes of reds and yellows there are
more sober harmonies of reds and blues – reds that tend to pink, and blues
that often verge on mauve and lilac. Frequently, as in *The Old Tree*, the
delectable whites and deep blacks give an effect of calm and deepen the
glow of the chromatism. His handling, too, is more sober than Vlaminck's.
Every brush-stroke blends better to give a general effect of more thick-laid
richness, thus creating a closer texture of pigment, with greater transparency
and an appearance of enamel. On the other hand, the drawing and arrangement acquire an importance which Vlaminck denies them. We see here the
close nervous precision of the contours, as well as an obvious concern with
composition. The diagonal formed by the leaning trunk of the tree is put in
contrast and steadied by that of the other tree boles. This introduces into
the small canvas a balance and stability that herald Derain's future experiments. His later development was to lead him to rally to the theories
of Cézanne, to profit by the influence of Negro art, to touch the fringes of
Cubism, to study medieval sculpture and finally, after 1919, to return to
traditional painting. Salon d'Automne, 1905 (No. 437). Purchased by the
Musées Nationaux, 1951.

EMILE-OTHON FRIESZ (1879–1949)
PORTRAIT OF FERNAND FLEURET

1907, signed and dated
Oil on canvas
Height 76 cm. (30″)
Width 60 cm. (23^1/$_2$″)

This is one of the most renowned of Friesz' works. Fernand Fleuret (1884
to 1943), a Norman like Friesz himself, was a writer of poetry and prose,
an art critic, an intimate friend of various artists (one of whom, Gimond,
has left a vivid portrait bust of him) – a personality in the world of letters
and the arts in Paris. However, the interest of this painting as a work of
art concerns us more than its value as a record: it is without any doubt
both a fine portrait and a superb painting. Admirable is the consummate
skill with which Friesz lays bare the mind and soul of his sitter: the choice
of pose and musing gesture; the gloomy black suit which gives a vague
suggestion of the macabre and at the same time emphasises the whiteness
of the long nervous hands and anxious face; the view of the subject from
above, bold and novel in a portrait, which deliberately calls attention to
the forehead and the top of the head, both, in any case, unusually large;
the setting for the figure, rather wretched and bare, giving a feeling of
solitariness and dejection; the slant of the composition's lines of force which
in some way corresponds to the poet's instability; the quiver in the very
brush-stroke which is similarly revealing: all these features combine to express Fleuret's troubled state of mind, almost as if even in 1907 Friesz has a
foreboding of his future insanity. But apart from his psychological insight
Friesz also shows himself to be a first-class painter and, above all, a
superlative colourist. The proof of this seems to lie in the skill with which
he lights up the central area of black by the reds, violets and mauves which
surround it, and so transmutes it into a colour, the most intense, the warmest
and most brilliant of the picture. But there are signs that this Fauve, intoxicated by violent tones, is beginning to calm down; the whites, always more
emphasised in his pictures than in those of his fellow-Fauves, now have
increased importance, and their ivory and creamy softness muffles, as it
were, the blare of the other tones. Moreover, the composition as a whole
displays a precision, a balance and a harmony that reveal in the Friesz of
1907 his feeling of the necessity for discipline and self-control, which was
soon to lead him to forsake Fauvism.

Purchased from the artist's widow by the Musées Nationaux, 1949.

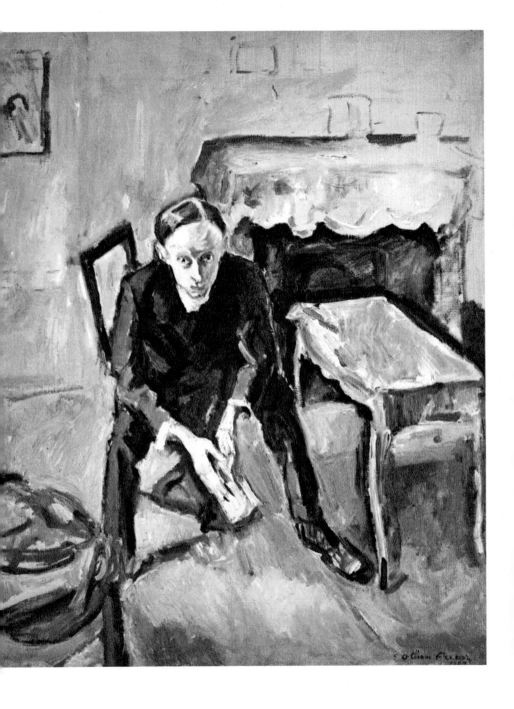

GEORGES BRAQUE (born 1882)   1906, signed
Landing stage of the harbour at l'Estaque   Oil on canvas
                                                             Height 37 cm. (15″)
                                                             Width 46 cm. (18″)

Braque did few paintings based, like this one, on the theories of Fauvism, to which he subscribed only in 1906 and 1907. It was painted in November 1906 (I have these facts from the artist himself), in the village of l'Estaque, to which he had been drawn by the presence of his friends and also by its association with Cézanne. This was his first visit to the Midi and he stayed no more than a few months.

The painting is typically Fauve. On the white ground, lightly primed with white lead, which shows through in several places, the painter has arranged touches of pure tones, never broken, never dingy: ultramarines, Prussian blues, lavender blues, emerald greens, Veronese greens, yellows, orange, vermilions, purples, pinks and violets. These interpret the iridescence of the water to perfection, and suggest explicitly the fishing boats, the houses, the woods dominated by the mountain, the clouds overhead and the evening sky. Colour, and colour alone, is supreme here. It defines or indicates the object, it expresses space and reproduces the light. Here, then, the Fauve idea is fully achieved.

But the true personality of Braque, still to emerge, is already discernible in this youthful Fauve work, revealed in the superlative accuracy that governs the setting of the planes, the indication of the volumes, the proportions, as well as the delicate and restrained lightness of the handling. Braque, from this time onwards, was to take as much pains to avoid violence and coarseness as his fellow painters in cultivating them. Furthermore, this picture, made up of touches of both pure and high tones, exhibits unexpectedly a quiet and sober harmony. Braque has given much space to the whites – of the canvas as well as paint – while in many places colours merely contribute the outline around their matt creaminess or crystal delicacy. These whites, at once ivory and silvery, impose their soft gleam on the work as a whole and give it the grace and subtle rarity we appreciate in Corot. Thus, all the qualities we come to expect from Braque are seen in full flower in this exquisite little picture.

Salon des Indépendants, 1907 (No. 723). Vollard Collection. Le Guillou Collection. Le Guillou Sale, Nantes, 1946. Purchased by the Musées Nationaux.

GEORGES BRAQUE (born 1882)   1911
Composition with ace of clubs   Oil, gouache and charcoal on canvas
                                                   Height 80 cm. (31^1/$_2$")
                                                    Width 59 cm. (23^1/$_4$")

This painting is the most characteristic example of analytical Cubism as practised by Braque and his followers from 1910 to 1912. All Cubists were then more and more taken up with the form of objects and the composition of the picture. Though they kept to accuracy of drawing (they were even said to use working designs) and to their washed-out chromatism, they were no longer satisfied merely to interpret form in a geometric sense. They had just become aware, on the one hand, that it resides in light and on the other, that it is not what the eye sees, so that certain problems arose. First, how could form exist in the atmosphere without being swallowed up by it? Second, how could it be represented not in its semblance but in its truth? They solved the first of these problems by infusing the light into the form and by identifying all the play of light with modifications of structure. The Cubists found their answer to the second problem after they had established the fact that things are never as we perceive them, in accordance with Braque's principle, 'the senses deform, but the mind forms.' From the hint given by Cézanne he created a system, and represented the various objects in his picture from the angle of least visual distortion. Here Braque looks down from above on the black table-top to avoid distortion by perspective and to show the whole structure of his subject. In order to see the drawer in the table, on the other hand, he has had to get in front of the table and slightly lower. He uses a downward view to show the playing-cards dealt out on a table and a horizontal view for the players, continually changing his position to get the view he needs. We find, however, that these processes, which aim at depicting the truth, create by their very novelty an image of reality likely to disconcert the uninitiated. The Cubist is over-realistic in the means he adopts, and he ends therefore by getting an un-realistic result.

   Other problems absorbed the Cubists also. There was that of combining several angles of vision at once, a very convenient way of disregarding perspective and of making real objects with their three dimensions come alive in the actual two dimensions of the picture. Still other means were used by them to arrive at the decorative element. In this typical still-life Braque has removed from the table the bunch of grapes and the plum that would naturally be on it and placed them in the upper part which looked as though it were going to be empty. The principle of all art with a decorative

GEORGES BRAQUE (born 1882)
WOMAN WITH GUITAR

1913, signed
Oil on canvas
Height 130 cm. (51")
Width 73 cm. (28³/₄")

This is one of the most celebrated and characteristic of the works painted by Braque on the eve of war in 1914. In it he remains faithful to the ideas which had inspired his analytical cubism. All the elements of Braque's earlier art form are to be found here: fragmentation of the figure and of objects by planes often identical with the play of light on the form; a combination of several simultaneous views; a structural working design; sober colours reinforced with blacks. But what is new in the work is a greater insistence on an accurate and illusionist rendering of the materials, and the wide use of letters representing printing type. It is not surprising that at the same time Braque – like Picasso – was using his first *papiers collés*. It was as if in face of the unrealistic results (despite the realistic intentions), both felt the need to keep contact with reality or the visible world, and used certain elements of it direct in their paintings.

In the Galerie Kahnweiler. Kahnweiler sale. Raoul La Roche Collection. Presented by M. Raoul La Roche, 1957.

Continued from page 136

aim – an evenly distributed lay-out of the canvas space – is applied by Braque here as in a number of his other works.

But we should not speak of the decorative in connection with the Cubists, who dread and despise it. They aim at difficulty of interpretation, since in their view this engenders poetry and human implications. 'To be too lucid is not becoming ... Seemliness asks for half-light to some degree,' declared Gleizes. Frequently the Cubists hint at objects rather than portray them, allowing us the pleasure of guessing what they may be. Thus, in this still-life the tall champagne glass in the centre is reduced to its right side and the left half of its base, a discretion which favours the poetic element. Presented by M. Paul Rosenberg, 1947.

138

GEORGES BRAQUE (born 1882)　　　　　　1937, signed and dated
THE DUET　　　　　　　　　　　　　　　　Oil on canvas
　　　　　　　　　　　　　　　　　　　Height 130 cm. (51″)
　　　　　　　　　　　　　　　　　　　Width 160 cm. (63″)
This work is one of a series of paintings, from 1936 to 1939, in which
Braque represents in his interiors people full face and in profile at the same
time. This meant reverting to a formula held in high regard by the Cubists
since 1911. But in this canvas, Braque has struck out further. Not only does
he confront the figures, but he integrates the setting with them. Here a
problem of grouping arises, boldly solved by opposing two symmetrical
figures on either side of a piano that forms the axis of the composition.
Colour, however, varies this symmetry, sombre on the right, higher and
more strident on the left. Braque Exhibition, Galerie Rosenberg (No. 16),
1937. Purchased by the State from the artist, 1938.

GEORGES BRAQUE (born 1882) 1945, signed
The Billiard Table Oil on canvas
Height 130 cm. (51″)
Width 194 cm. (76¹/₂″)

The only painter who remained loyal to Cubism for his whole lifetime was
Braque, the supreme Cubist (Juan Gris, of course, died too young to have
been a deserter from the Cubist ranks). It is therefore not surprising to
find in this work of his old age several characteristics of Braque's Cubist
manner of more than thirty years earlier. He still represents the object
from different angles, so as to present as complete an image as possible: the
billiard table is shown to the right as it appears to the player standing
before it, but to the left as if seen by the player bending over it to play.
Braque introduces the time element by juxtaposing the successive images of
an object, and by representing on the billiard table the luminous tracks of
the rolling balls. Both vision and manner remain Cubist; the paint incorpo-
rates materials extraneous to painting; formerly it was *papier collé* but

141

PABLO PICASSO (born 1881)　　　　　　　　　1905, signed
Seated Nude　　　　　　　　　　　　　　　　　Oil on cardboard
　　　　　　　　　　　　　　　　　　　　Height 106 cm. (41³/₄″)
　　　　　　　　　　　　　　　　　　　　Width 76 cm. (30″)

This first-rate example of Picasso's Blue period (1902 to 1905) is all the more moving because the artist has purposely left it incomplete. It is not easy to see what useful addition could have been made to a picture so near to perfection. The line, light and incisive, has a purity and music that puts Picasso, beside Ingres and Botticelli, among the greatest virtuosos of melodic drawing. The palette is quiet and accurate and brings together the blues and the greys, and even the ochres used for priming, with a subtlety at once delicate and forceful. The drawing combines both nervous vigour and languor. What poignancy is conveyed by this thin figure, where the hardened sickly look of the flesh is in keeping with the melancholy distress reflected in the face!

Gertrude Stein Collection, Paris. Pierre Matisse Gallery, New York. Walter P. Chrysler Collection, New York. Purchased by the Musées Nationaux, 1954.

Continued from page 141

here it is sand, which gives a pleasing texture to the pigment. We can unreservedly admire the faultless workmanship, the quiet full colouring, and the mastery with which the rectilinears of the billiard table are contrasted with the wavy lines of the plant and the curves of vase and pedestal table. This subtle, sober treatment is a measure of the painter's deep sympathy with things in themselves, which to him are more than mere inanimate objects.

Purchased from the artist by the Musées Nationaux, 1946.

PABLO PICASSO (born 1881)   1925
THE DRESSMAKER'S WORK-ROOM   Oil on canvas
                                                   Height 172 cm. (67³/₄″)
                                                    Width 265 cm. (104″)

Picasso, who had been living at 26, rue de la Boétie since 1918, had only
to look across the street to see a smart little dress-shop, the inspiration for
this picture. He has painted a triptych: on the right we see someone
entering the shop; in the centre there are a customer and a saleswoman;
on the left a milliner makes a hat. However, Picasso does not convey his
feelings by giving a precise and anecdotal representation, but uses the more
subtle means of colour and even more of rhythm. The grey monochrome,
light and delicate, harmonises with the flat curves that wind across the
whole picture and impart to it a light surface movement. The artist seems
to endow the reality he presents with a sort of musical counterpoise,
fulfilling Apollinaire's prophecy: 'Painting of the future will be to that of
yesterday what music is to literature.' Presented by the artist, 1947.

PABLO PICASSO (born 1881)   1942
L'AUBADE   Oil on canvas

Height 195 cm. (76³/₄")

Width 265 cm. (104")

The most telling sign of the degree of Picasso's obsession with traditional painting is not to be found in his 'classical' pictures, but rather in paintings such as *L'Aubade*, where he sets out to make his own comments on great paintings of the past. In this case, it is Titian's *Venus listening to Music*, which he had seen in the Prado. Here we have the same subject, the same composition – though Picasso eliminates the setting with his characteristic distaste for landscape – but not precisely the same aesthetic. From Cubism comes the combining of several angles of view. It is to Surrealism he owes the metamorphosis of the guitar-player into a kind of totem crowned with mask. At the same time *L'Aubade* shows Picasso's inventiveness and originality, his taste for the monstrous and the fantastic, the authority of his drawing,

Continued on page 148

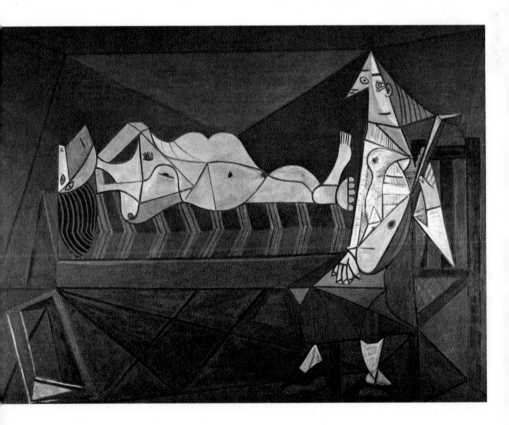

PABLO PICASSO (born 1881)   1936
STILL-LIFE WITH A LEMON AND ORANGES   Oil on canvas
Height 54 cm. (21¹/₄″)
Width 65 cm. (25¹/₂″)

Picasso, a Proteus of contemporary painting, has developed one style after another, all to a high degree different. But even more surprisingly, he often works in dissimilar forms simultaneously, and alongside canvases of such violence as *The Enamel Saucepan,* has painted others with all the mildness of *Still-life with a lemon and oranges.* The drawing is flexible, with curves and ellipses dominating; the tones are subdued, muted, with a soft and silky gleam. The light is filtered and looks phosphorescent, the paint is sparing, the handling delicate. All these features give this little picture a studied elegance that shows the almost limitless variety of Picasso's inspiration and artistry. Presented by the artist in 1947.

PABLO PICASSO (born 1881) 1945, dated
THE ENAMEL SAUCEPAN Oil on canvas
Height 82 cm. (32¹/₄")
Width 106,5 cm. (42")

No picture better displays Picasso's supremely powerful imagination. He
regards utterly commonplace objects, submits them to a metamorphosis and
brings forth a poetic image that stirs the heart. The Surrealists have never
been able to bring about such a transformation. His success is to be explained
by his unerring mastery – a mastery such as no Surrealist could claim. We
see it here, especially in the fiery violence of the drawing, the ardour of
the colour, the almost unbridled force of the brush-stroke and the extraordinary powerfulness of the form. Presented by the artist, 1947.

ALBERT GLEIZES (1881–1953)
LANDSCAPE

1911, signed and dated
Oil on canvas
Height 147 cm. (58″)
Width 115 cm. (45¼″)

Picasso and Braque were the originators and leaders of Cubism, but other painters besides those who gravitated around them came to similar conclusions at the same time, and also propounded the geometric rendering of nature in order to restore to natural objects their three-dimensional character, and to ensure that the picture was given a vigorous structure. Among these was Gleizes. This landscape owes to Cézanne the reduction of shapes to simple volumes, obvious to the understanding and therefore forceful, and the extremely rigorous arrangement of the composition. But, following Picasso and Braque, Gleizes drew away from Cézanne as far as colour was concerned. While Cézanne loved vivid and light-reflecting colour, Gleizes preferred it lustreless and, as it were, washed-out, proof against conveying any impression of light. It seems as if the Cubists – showing greater fidelity to the spirit, at least, of Seurat than to the example of Cézanne – were concerned to solve the problem of the structure of shapes and of the picture as a whole before they tackled that of colour and light.

Salon des Indépendants, 1911 (No. 2613). Received from the Commission de Récupération Artistique, 1949.

Continued from page 145

his harsh colour-scale, acid in the high tones (greens and violets), thick and full in the earth-colours, the powerful and incised expression of form, his imagination and the wealth of his culture as an artist. Salon d'Automne, 1944 (No. 49). Presented by the artist, 1947.

MARCEL DUCHAMP (born 1887)
THE CHESS PLAYERS

1911, signed and dated
Height 50 cm. (19¹/₂″)
Width 61 cm. (24″)

It is from Cubism that Marcel Duchamp derives, at any rate at the time of *The Chess Players*. It is his sole work in a French public collection, or even perhaps in a European one, for almost his whole output (cut short early and in any case extremely limited) is in the United States. This work, by all the evidence, was influenced by Cézanne's *Card Players*, to which Duchamp refers for his theme. Nevertheless the work contains differences that reveal the temperament of the painter. There is the difference in subject, which indicates Duchamp's passion for chess (this finally made him abandon painting, and became his chief preoccupation in life). Then there is the difference in technique, in which the effect on him of Cubism becomes apparent: the structure of the figures, for instance, suggested rather than portrayed; the very sober chromatism, confined to earth colours and grey lightened by some pinks and 'steadied' by two black bands that mount vertically at the sides of the canvas. A further difference lies in the handling, at once delicate and firm – and also in the polished execution. The sum of all these elements makes a Cubist painting of this work. This is not surprising, since the studio of Duchamp's brothers, Jacques Villon and Raymond Duchamp-Villon, (where Gleizes, Metzinger, Picabia, La Fresnaye, Léger and Kupka used to foregather), was one of the starting-points of the movement and, indeed, one of its 'high places'. But a Cubism rather different from that of the Bateau Lavoir of Picasso and Braque developed here, one in some respects more subtle. This is clearly seen in *The Chess Players*, in the calligraphy which has something in common with Italian Futurism (which this work anticipates), and in the dissociation of the shapes and the strange 'over-print' that the artist uses to make us aware of the concentrated thought of the players. The time was not far off when he was to paint his *Nude descending a staircase* (1912) and his well-known *Bride stripped by her bachelors, even* (between 1915 and 1923) – both forerunners of Dadaism.

In the Salon de la Section d'Or, 1912. Jacques Villon Collection. Cubist exhibition, Musée National d'Art Moderne, 1953 (No. 62). Purchased from Jacques Villon by the Musées Nationaux, 1955.

LOUIS MARCOUSSIS (1883–1941)
STILL-LIFE WITH DRAUGHT-BOARD

1912, signed and dated
Oil on canvas
Height 139 cm. (54³/₄″)
Width 93 cm. (36¹/₂″)

Louis Markous took the pseudonym of Marcoussis on the advice of his friend Apollinaire. He came to Cubism towards 1911 and was drawn with Juan Gris into the orbit of Picasso and Braque. And in the company of Gris, Modigliani, the critic Maurice Raynal and Princet the mathematician, who had a passion for Cubism, he was often to be found at the little café in Montmartre 'Chez l'ami Emile'. In 1912 both he and Juan Gris did some decorations for the café. One of these, after changing hands several times, came to the Musée d'Art Moderne, where it serves as a wonderful example of analytical Cubism as practised by this painter during the period 1911–1913. The structural working design, the *camaïeu* of sober colour with ochres as a base, the quiet and harmonious treatment, the careful structure, a combination of several angles of vision – these are the elements that should be noticed in this still-life. It is a work where the individuality of the artist is revealed in the unusual fastidiousness of the chromatism, in the oiliness of the pigment, in the precision of the light, in the graceful arrangement of the objects across the canvas, and in the combination of delicate appeal and subtlety of feeling.

Painted for the café 'Chez l'ami Emile', Place Ravignan. Private Collection, Senlis. Paul Guillaume Collection. Albert Sarraut Collection. Henriette Gomez Collection. Purchased by the Musées Nationaux, 1950.

152

JUAN GRIS, real name José Gonzalez (1887–1927) 1917

<small>Still-life on a chair</small> Oil on canvas

Height 101 cm. (39³/₄")

Width 73 cm. (28³/₄")

No other Cubist represented the movement so perfectly as this artist. Whether he would have gone on to other horizons had he not died prematurely is, indeed, questionable, so much was he at ease in a world whose foundations he had no hand in laying and yet whose language he could use so well. (He only came to Cubism in 1911, whereas Picasso and Braque had started in 1907.) All the expedients of Cubism are applied here with the assurance of someone strong in theory, whose assiduous practice achieved a flawless style.

We have here fragmentation and geometric crystallisation of the object, the use of several angles of vision, a structural working design, sober and austere colour. Furthermore, the handling is so impersonal as to be illusionist in portraying materials – note the artifical wood of the parquet, the strict arrangement of the shapes within a composition carefully thought out and given a masterly balance. All these elements make this picture a typical instance of the 'synthetic Cubism' fostered by Picasso and Juan Gris during 1913–14. Still, the character and temperament of Juan Gris do not limit him to embodying Cubism; they also have particular qualities that give this still-life an implicit dignity. There is a scornful refusal of anything easily appealing and a preference for the most exacting economy – even in the choice of motif; there are, too, a natural dryness and severity, a stripping bare and even asceticism. The whole of Juan Gris' inner nature is here revealed, and one of its most engaging virtues is that its very faults and limitations go towards working out an art which thereby achieves a noble stature.

In the Galerie Rosenberg. Raoul La Roche Collection. Presented by M. Raoul La Roche, 1952.

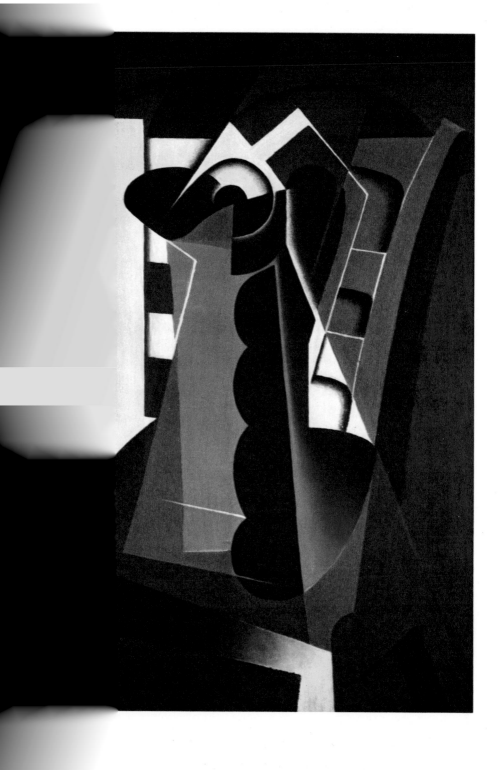

JEAN METZINGER (1883–1956)
LANDSCAPE

c. 1920, signed
Oil on canvas
Height 80 cm. (31¹/₂")
Width 65 cm. (25¹/₂")

Besides the Cubists who were gathered about Picasso and Braque, there were painters who pursued similar experiments independently and, perhaps, got more rebuffs because they exhibited more in successive Salons d'Automne and Salons des Indépendants. Gleizes and Metzinger must be given pride of place amongst these 'other' Cubists if only because they formulated the principles of the new school – and this a year in advance of Apollinaire whose *Peintres cubistes* appeared in 1914. It was in fact in 1913 that their joint work *Du Cubisme* was published. And at the same time a whole series of large paintings revealed the youthful and defiant talent of Metzinger to the visitors to the Salons: *Le Gouter* (1911), *En Canot* (1913), *L'Oiseau bleu* (1913) – the Musée d'Art Moderne is fortunate to have acquired the splendid studies for these pictures. The painter is not so intrepid as Picasso or Braque in analysing and fragmenting form and building it up again, but he is more ambitious in his choice of subjects and in his efforts to construct vast rhythmic groupings on a strict plan. These features of his art, firmly adopted even before 1914, continue to appear after 1919, as in this enchanting *Landscape*. The handling has a fleecy look, the light is silvery, the colour-range pale and limpid with faded greens as a base; the line has many more curves than in the work he did between 1910 and 1914. These characteristics taken together make it possible to assign this undated painting to about 1920, to Metzinger's second Cubist period. While he still keeps to the methods he developed during his first Cubist period, he applies them to an art of more realism. Even so, he is always concerned to let his quiet and measured sensibility have its way and to paint in the sober, delicate and distinguished style which makes him one of the most exquisite of the minor poets of Cubist painting.

In the Rosenberg Collection, Livengood Collection. Presented by the Societé des Amis du Musée d'Art Moderne, 1958.

FERNAND LÉGER (1881–1955)   1911–1912, signed
THE WEDDING   Oil on canvas
                                              Height 275 cm. (108¼″)
                                               Width 206 cm. (81″)

This is Fernand Léger's masterpiece in the Cubist style, and we see here
how he is related to Braque, Picasso and the orthodox Cubists in the
accuracy of the drawing, the whole style of the finished design, the colour,
quiet and in a low key, the bronze *camaïeu* with a base of earth colours
and ochres, broken with some greens, olive, a faded blue and a faint pink.
The analysis of the form, in which he is absorbed, the breaking up of the
figures of people into geometric volumes, one fitting into another, as well
as the various angles of view that he uses – these also associate the picture
with analytical Cubism. But the familiar subject (the strict Cubists would
have called it anecdotal), the movement that carries the wedding along
the village street, are evidence of preoccupations foreign to the Cubists and
perhaps more ambitious than theirs. Léger is no longer concerned merely
to analyse and then reconstruct the static object of a still-life, serenely-posed
model or landscape. Rather, he takes life itself, with its movement, its
complex gathering of individuals contained within a particular framework,
for his theme. The picture is thus on the same lines as La Fresnaye's *Artillery*
(1910–1911) or Marcel Duchamp's *Nude descending a staircase* (1912), and
also as the works of the Italian Futurists, which, exhibited in the Bernheim
Gallery in February 1912, were to bring their theories and achievements
to the notice of Paris. But he was already creating his personal art-form,
one that gave promise of the future Léger and in which his genius proves
itself more alive than Picasso's or Braque's to the force of vitality and the
phenomenon of dynamism, and indeed to all that goes to make up the
grandeur of human existence. Implicit, too, in his *Wedding* of 1911 is the
Léger who, a little later, will try in his *Contrast in forms* to convey the
vibration of things, who will be painting in his 'Dynamic style' throughout
the war years 1914–1918, and who, from 1945 onwards, will be setting
himself to discover a sublime and yet contemporary interpretation of
features of everyday life.

    At the Salon des Indépendants, 1912 (No. 3498). Presented by Alfred
Flechtheim, 1937. Musée du Luxembourg.

FERNAND LÉGER (1881–1955) 1913, signed and dated
CONTRAST IN FORMS Oil on canvas
Height 100 cm. (39^1/$_2$")
Width 81 cm. (32")

Léger, like Delaunay and like the Italian Futurists, felt the impact of the dynamism of modern civilization, and saw the machine as the most significant expression of that dynamic quality. In 1913–1914 he painted a series of canvases in which, by telescoping simple volumes into one another, he sought to set up contrasts among them; by the same means, in a way that might be called absolute, he tried to give an exact idea of these machines by suggesting their complex construction and the force of their rhythmic beat. The series was called by Léger '*Contrast in forms*', and this picture is a good sample. One is struck by the severity and the simplicity of the volumes, more often than not cylindrical or conic – 'Tubism' was the term used at this time – and they leave an impression of austere power. And then, the consistent use of discontinuity is striking in the drawing, the colour, the lay-out of the shapes and the general arrangement of the picture – all used by the artist to indicate very clearly the jerky movement of the machine. By this concern for the dynamic and his vivid palette, Léger turns his back on the Cubists and enters the camp of the Futurists and of the German painters of the *Blaue Reiter*.

The painting was in the Galerie Kahnweiler. Kahnweiler Sale. André Lefèvre Collection. Presented by M. and Mme André Lefèvre.

ROGER DE LA FRESNAYE (1885–1925)   c. 1907
SELF-PORTRAIT   Oil on canvas
Height 81 cm. (32″)
Width 65 cm. (25¹/₂″)

This self-portrait is a work of La Fresnaye's youth and shows how much he profited at the Académie Ranson by the teaching of such masters as Maurice Denis and Sérusier. The colour has the subtle restraint of the Nabi palette and the light brings out the same filtered elusiveness that we find in Vuillard, whose intimist poetry is also present in this canvas. Later, the influence of Cézanne and then of the Cubists was to take La Fresnaye along more ambitious paths; but he was to keep throughout some of the qualities he shows already in this portrait, and even give them greater point. There is the polished drawing, the exquisite appropriateness of the colour, and the studied handling – all characteristics that are not surprising when one has once seen this intelligent, aristocratic face. La Fresnaye had a great curiosity about his own personality. He made two studies (in 1905 and 1908) before painting this version, and was to paint many more self-portraits, especially towards the end of his life when, having been gassed in the war and become tubercular, he followed, brush in hand, the inroads of the disease and the suffering he endured. It would be hard to find anything more distressing in the whole of contemporary painting than this series of impressions of his own likeness (there must be about half-a-dozen), where sheet by sheet, death is seen strengthening its hold on a man of perception, breeding and high courage, who looks at the image of himself with detachment and a stoic endurance, blended with Christian serenity.

Purchased by the Musées Nationaux in 1935.

ROGER DE LA FRESNAYE (1885–1925)   1910, signed
THE CUIRASSIER   Oil on canvas
                                      Height 180 cm. (71″)
                                       Width 180 cm. (71″)
Here La Fresnaye 'restates' Géricault's well-known *Wounded Cuirassier* in
the language of Cézanne. He geometricises the shapes in order to bring out
their innate force, and to the same end cuts out all detail. The lines of force
are accentuated to contrast strongly the impetus of the man towards the
right and of the animal towards the left; the balance comes from their oppo-
sition. Fresnaye's Cubism thus differs from that of Braque and Picasso and
relates him to the Italian Futurists, whom he anticipates. Salon des Indépendants, 1911 (No. 2400). Purchased by the Musée Nationaux.

ROGER DE LA FRESNAYE (1885–1925)
Seated Man

1913
Oil on canvas
Height 130 cm. (51″)
Width 165 cm. (65″)

Roger de La Fresnaye seceded from Cubism, and stands to it as Seurat does to Impressionism. Seurat wanted to add solidity of form and composition to the Impressionists' play of light, La Fresnaye set himself to complete the Cubist structure by expressing light, air and atmosphere by means of colour. After 1913 he abandoned the still-lifes of cubism for open-air scenes such as this. In place of the bleak, muted colour-scale he has one that is vivid, fresh and sunlit. The light touch is made to give an airy look to objects. But these results are not obtained at the expense of composition, or of the severely-drawn shapes enclosed in a pure contour. Collection of M. Paul Petit. Purchased by the Musées Nationaux, 1957.

JACQUES VILLON (Gaston Duchamp) (born 1875)
PORTRAIT OF RAYMOND DUCHAMP-VILLON
1911, signed
and dated
Oil on wood
Height 35 cm. (13³/₄")
Width 26,5 cm. (10⁴")

Jacques Villon, whose real name was Gaston Duchamp, had spent many long years doing humorous drawings before coming to Cubism about 1911 through his young brother Marcel Duchamp. He was to use this method thereafter with uncommon originality. As a good Norman, he responded to the art of his famous fellow-Norman Claude Monet and he was, as he himself expressed it, 'the Impressionist Cubist'. Still, he was 'the futurist Cubist' too, one of the Cubists who tried to introduce into the wholly static world of Picasso and Braque the movement that the Italian Futurists were then making the chief aim of their experiments. Also, he was the Cubist who paid most attention to the portrayal of the mind and soul of his subjects, and it is not generally appreciated that his achievements in portrait painting, especially self-portraits, are the richest in style and the most convincing. Certainly this is at once apparent from the portrait of his younger brother – Raymond Duchamp-Villon (1876–1918), a first-rate sculptor whose career was cut short by the war but whose work, even so, belongs to the most distinguished *avant-garde* sculpture of the time. No one will dispute that several Cubists, notably Picasso, painted splendid portraits during the period 1908–1914. Still, those portraits are more studies of shapes than excursions into psychology. It is quite otherwise in this painting, where Jacques Villon has succeeded in portraying the secret springs of an unusually gifted personality – moved by his very deep attachment to this brother, who shared his studio at Puteaux. The brothers were the leading spirits of gatherings at Puteaux, whose importance for the development of modern painting, though long disregarded, is considerable.

In the Jacques Villon Exhibition, Musée National d'Art Moderne, 1951 (No. 4). Cubist Exhibition (No. 78). Presented by the artist, 1953.

JACQUES VILLON (Gaston Duchamp) (born 1875)   1949, signed
LE SCRIBE   Oil on canvas
                                                          Height 92 cm. (36$^1/_4$")
                                                          Width 75 cm. (29$^1/_2$")

The attempt of La Fresnaye to blend Cubism with Impressionism was taken up and developed by Jacques Villon who, on his own account, tried to reconcile figurative with abstract art. In this self-portrait (Villon often took himself for a model) we can appreciate the purity of the colour, its luminosity, its soft and silky brilliance, the subtle discrimination that has led the artist to place next to one another two zones of different blues without loss of effect, as well as two different greens. The incisive lightness of the drawing reminds us that the painter was equally distinguished as an engraver.

It will be seen how the delicate interpretation, so full of character and implication, lays bare the mind and soul of the man. It is matched by the strict over-all arrangement of the picture, a construction based on great still areas which are brought together with as much nobility and grace, splendour of design that is yet close to nature, allied to intelligence and depth of feeling, as we find in the fine stretches of water and the *parterres* of a garden in the French manner. One cannot imagine a painting more typically French than this portrait, made up of musing, informality and restraint, and all pervaded by a smile.

The picture was purchased from the artist by the State in 1949.

JACQUES VILLON (Gaston Duchamp) (born 1875)   1949, signed
BETWEEN TOULOUSE AND ALBI   and dated
Oil on canvas
Height 54 cm. (21$^{1}/_{4}''$)
Width 78 cm. (30$^{3}/_{4}''$)

Like Roger de La Fresnaye, with whom he had close ties, Jacques Villon
dreamed of fusing Cubism and Impressionism; how successful he was can
be seen in this landscape, painted at the time of the movement south in
1941, in the face of the German occupation, when he had taken refuge with
friends living near Gaillac. The choice of subject, the feeling of space, of
light and atmosphere and the pale tender colour are all clear signs of
Impressionist influence upon Villon – a Norman like Boudin and Monet.
There is no trace here, however, of the disdain for form and composition
which Monet, Sisley and Pissarro had come to by too exclusive a love for
light and for optical sensation. Very accurate drawing reminds us that
Villon excelled in engraving; it defines the shapes, emphasizes the planes
and even creates distance. One notices immediately the very clear arrangement, based on three triangles: two right-angled triangles touching at their
lower acute angles and enclosing between them an isosceles triangle sur-
mounted by a long quadrilateral. It is from this lucid design that the feeling
of balance, precision and purity in this painting derives. This is a characteristic example of the art of Villon, which is so carefully considered, so
sensitive and pure that it is best described as 'after the manner of Racine'.
In the Salon d'Automne 1941 (No. 2141). Purchased by the State.

FRANZ KUPKA (1871–1957)
PLANES BY COLOURS

1910–1911, signed and dated
Oil on canvas
Height 110 cm. (43¹/₄″)
Width 110 cm. (43¹/₄″)

Kupka, a Czech, had his training in art at the academy of modern painting in Vienna. Then in 1894 he came to Paris, where he was to spend the rest of his life. He took up illustration in the style of Toulouse-Lautrec and later painted in the Fauve manner, before passing on in 1911 to abstract art, of which he was a pioneer, along with Picabia, Delaunay and his wife in Paris, and Kandinsky in Munich. The study of a woman which he called *Planes by colours* was painted at the stage when he gave up the figurative for abstraction. The figure is still quite recognisable in the picture but it is clear that it is no more than a pretext for a chromatic structure. Where did Kupka get the idea of transferring people and objects from the plane of reality to that of abstract creation? The answer is certainly: from the Viennese painter Klimt, who was the foremost advocate in Austria of the *Jugendstil*, corresponding to *art nouveau* of Paris. By that time Klimt was in fact expressing himself in strange, mannered and sophisticated compositions. These transformed women in Viennese society (the chief subjects of his painting) into kinds of Far Eastern idols, where the rippling line, the variegations of delicate splashes of colour and the flattening, all contributed perfectly to a decorative whole.

Kupka kept the unusual colour-scale of the *Jugendstil* as well as the drawing, exact and yet elusive, and the general decorative character. He only had to add to these features something of the quality of music to free himself still more from the shackles of reality and get nearer to the line that divides figurative from abstract art – a line that he was shortly afterwards to cross so resolutely.

In the Salon d'Automne, 1911 (No. 811). Purchased from the artist's widow by the Musées Nationaux, 1957.

172

FRANZ KUPKA (1871–1957) 1911–1912, signed and dated
Étude par la fugue Oil on canvas
Height 66 cm. (26")
Width 66 cm. (26")

At the Salon d'Automne of 1912, Kupka exhibited *Amorpha, Fugue in two colours,* which hangs today in the National Gallery of Prague. The Musée d'Art Moderne has a study for it which is perhaps even more remarkable, since it is free of the rather decorative element and *art nouveau* tone that mark the definitive work. In this study, by contrast, the main features are a severity and a quality of music, produced by the colour, muted, quiet and delicate and by the supple and firm rhythm. Curves and ellipses give this painting a certain movement, but it is nevertheless far removed from the art of Delaunay and his wife, which is wholly dynamic, surging and even explosive. It is at once more concentrated, grave and unadorned, and is a promise of the bare, austere paintings Kupka went on to do some months later, when he used only simple and geometric shapes, oblong rectangles or trapeziums – a typical example is *Vertical planes No. 1* (1912) in the Musée d'Art Moderne. All goes to show that Kupka was again in the lead when abstract art was swinging towards a geometric concept, order, discipline, bareness and the ascetic. In that respect he anticipated Malevitch, whose first pictures in this vein date from 1913, and was even further ahead of Mondrian and the Dutch Neo-Plastic artists, who only came to these formulas in 1915 or 1916. Geometric abstraction was acclaimed in the Netherlands and took root also in Germany, where it was to gain enough ascendancy at the *Bauhaus* of Weimar to influence Kandinsky himself to rally to its theories. Kupka's vital part in this movement is thus clearly to be seen. In justice, then, he must be accorded a place beside Picabia, the Delaunays and Kandinsky among the originators of abstract painting, and also close to Malevitch as one of those responsible for the crystallizing of abstraction.

The painting was purchased from the artist's widow by the Musées Nationaux in 1957.

174

ROBERT DELAUNAY (1885–1941)
A WINDOW

1912–1913, signed and dated
Oil on canvas
Height 111 cm. (43³/₄")
Width 90 cm. (35¹/₂")

Robert Delaunay had been caught up for a short time by Cubism, which was entirely against his natural bent as a lyric colourist. But in 1912 he returned to the enthusiasm for extremely luminous and dynamic colour that had possessed him in his youth. He was, however, to use colour quite differently from the Impressionists and the Fauves: his aim was to make it, in some way, the very purpose of his picture, without the least concern for representation. This means that in Orphic Cubism – a movement inspired by Delaunay and given its name by Apollinaire in 1913 – we see one of the first indications of abstract art. As we look at this particular canvas, we do indeed cross the Rubicon with the artist. The figurative element is not entirely lacking: one may still identify – or perhaps guess at – the stir of the muslin curtains at the window and beyond it, discern the outline of the Eiffel Tower, which the artist never tired of acclaiming in his pictures. However, this is evidently not the true subject of the painting, which has no *raison d'être* but Delaunay's aim to heighten the colour of the light filtered through the window-pane and curtains and thus broken up into tones that exist in their own right – absolutely, so to speak. The painting is a symphony of reds, pinks, orange, yellows, greens, laid on in fluid and rhythmic waves. With its superb lyricism it inspired one of Apollinaire's most famous poems.

The painting was purchased by the Musées Nationaux from Mme Delaunay in 1950.

ROBERT DELAUNAY (1885–1941)   1913–1922
LE MANÈGE DE COCHONS   Oil on canvas
Height 250 cm. (98¹/₂″)
Width 250 cm. (98¹/₂″)

As Delaunay was so responsive to the 'modern spirit', to colour and movement, it is not surprising that he should have been taken with the sight of
merry-go-rounds. He used this theme in 1906 and again in 1913 before
painting this final version, which reflects the influence of Toulouse-Lautrec
and his well-known *Baraque de la Goulue*, in which one of the decorative
panels has a similar composition. Few of Delaunay's works represent him
so completely as this canvas. The man absorbed by reality appears here
alongside the man drawn by the 'non-objective'. The one is revealed in
the portrayal of the pigs of the merry-go-round, by the presence in the
centre of the composition of two legs wearing black stockings and below,
of a tall hat, and especially by the portrait of the poet Tristan Tzara in
the foreground. On the other hand the multi-coloured circles which make
up the greater part of the canvas bring to mind the Delaunay who in 1912
and 1913 had painted the *Circular forms*, and foreshadow the artist who in
1930 was to paint *Joie de Vivre*.

The 'constant' that is most personal to him is certainly the multi-coloured
circle that he favours to the point of obsession. It is seen first in 1906
in *Landscape with disk*. It appears again as cast by the light filtering through
stained glass on the floor of the *Saint-Séverin* of 1908. At the same time
abstract and intended to portray the globe of the world, these circles are
paramount in the *Circular forms* series and the different versions of the
Homage to Blériot, where they indicate not only the propeller of the
aeroplane and its rotation breaking up the light into all the colours of
the spectrum, but also the earth's motion, the triumphant power of aeronautics and even the actual lay-out of the composition. It is the same with
the *Portuguese Still-lifes* of 1915–1916, where the vegetables, fruit, jugs
and figures of women tend to be mere multi-coloured circles. No wonder,
then, that Delaunay has rendered the turning of the wooden pigs by polychrome circles, and that they seem to lift us off our feet into the deafening
whirligig of the merry-go-round.

We see in the *Manège de Cochons* not only the composer caught up
by the rhythmic and delirious movement, but the colourist too, delighting
in making all the colours of the rainbow ripple and offset one another. It
is indeed a sumptuous blaze of fireworks, its brilliance increased by transparency, giving a radiant luminosity. With the black stockings as the dark

central core of the composition, the colours are fused to right and left, laid on liberally and with lyric elation, truly in harmony with the genius of the painter.

In the Galerie Guillaume, 1922. Salon des Indépendants, 1923 (No. 1270, title *Manège électrique*). Retrospective Delaunay Exhibition, Musée National d'Art Moderne, 1958 (No. 65). Presented by Mme Sonia Delaunay, 1958.

ROBERT DELAUNAY (1885–1941)
THE CITY OF PARIS
　　　　　1910–1912, signed and dated
　　　　　　　　　Oil on canvas
　　　　　　　Height 267 cm. (105″)
　　　　　　Width 406 cm. (159½″)

This large composition, which Apollinaire declared the most important canvas of the Salon, is both the culmination and the finish of Robert Delaunay's Cubist manner. In 1909–1910 he was influenced by Cézanne and painted in a Cézanne-Cubist style, like Picasso, Braque, Léger, Gleizes, La Fresnaye and others at that time. He portrays houses and nudes geometrically, states firmly the structure of the form and the painting as a whole, and aims at a bare precision of line. But his love of colour (which had attracted him to Neo-Impressionism about 1905–1908), reappears in this canvas after its eclipse in the *Cities* series (1910), hence a scale of colours that are not the sparing and muted tones of the Cubists. This was the first divergence, but a second came through his passion for the dynamic, which was wholly contrary to their feeling for static art. The sign of this passion is the introduction of an Eiffel Tower, which for Delaunay was and would always be the very symbol of modern civilization – a civilization that he saw as dynamic in its essence. It will be noticed too that instead of painting a precise image of this monument, Delaunay prefers to define the spirit of it by interpreting its thrust and strength. Thus, he takes his stand as the forerunner of Italian Futurism and at the

180

same time, by his vivid colour, so transparent and flowing, he anticipates
the art of Paul Klee, Franz Marc, August Macke and similiar artists, on
whom he exercised considerable influence between 1912 and 1914. Salon
des Indépendants, 1912 (No. 868). Armory Show, 1913. Purchased from
the artist by the State.

SONIA DELAUNAY (born 1885)
ELECTRIC PRISMS

1914, signed and dated
Oil on canvas
Height 250 cm. (98¹/₂″)
Width 250 cm. (98¹/₂″)

Robert and Sonia Delaunay, husband and wife, worked together in close unison of heart and mind, and as they were carrying out parallel experiments at the same time it was not possible to tell which of the two had been the originator. Thus, they arrived at Orphic Cubism simultaneously, and so at abstract painting, to which belong Robert Delaunay's *The Window* and Sonia Delaunay's *La Prose du Trans-Sibérien et de la petite Jehanne de France* (1913), one of the earliest essays in abstract art, her *Le Coffret,* shown at the Herbstsalon in Berlin 1913, and the *Bal Bulbier* (1913), one of the most splendid and characteristic of Orphic Cubist paintings. At the Salon des Indépendants of 1914 the Delaunays exhibited two large compositions, both in the same vein: Robert's *Homage to Blériot* and Sonia's *Electric prisms.* The two works have much in common, for instance the large size of canvas, brilliant chromatism and the spirit informing them – a spirit which rests on the boundary between the figurative and the 'non-objective', as they term it, the figurative being more easily discerned in Delaunay's canvas and the 'non-objective' in that of Sonia. The same passion for the dynamic comes through in both works, and is seen best in the structure of the composition built on curves and ellipses, which give the effect of strong flowing movement, as in the *Disks* and *Circular Forms,* where Delaunay succeeded so well in conveying the life-beat of the universe. The contrast of the colours here, added to their transparent and luminous quality, increase still further the impression of a force welling up from within the picture. Yet there is no motley of gaudy colour, no jangle of noise; in spite of the intensity and variety of the colours, their pervading luminosity fuses them into a whole and provides the harmony.

In the Salon des Indépendants, 1914, Catalogue No. 3135. Cubist Exhibition, Musée National d'Art Moderne, Catalogue No. 231. Purchased from the artist by the State, 1958.

FRANCIS PICABIA (1879–1953)
Udnie, (American girl, or The Dance)

1913, signed
Oil on canvas
Height 300 cm. (118″)
Width 300 cm. (118″)

Picabia was the originator of abstract painting, and the first demonstration of it was his *Rubber* (Musée d'Art Moderne), a water-colour painted in Paris 1908–1909, a year before the first abstract paintings of Kandinsky at Munich. During the years 1910 to 1912 he forsook abstraction for Cubism and the more dynamic art of the *Section d'Or*. But he returned to abstract painting again in 1913 with some large canvases, the most striking of them inspired by the dancing of a ballerina travelling on a liner from New York to Le Havre in 1913. In this picture he has tried to express the rhythmic swirl of the dancer by non-figurative shapes.

The great diagonal stretching from the lower right corner to the upper left, the placing on the inside of this oblique band of elements united by a spiral, the connexions and the breaks among the coloured planes thus assembled – all serve to translate the choreographic evolutions of this artist, whom Picabia has named Udnie. He mingles subtlety (the greys) and clear statement (the greens), so that the colour, by turns muted (the blues) and limpid (the whites), corresponds to the accompanying music. With what freedom and invention, charm and vitality and with what boldness (note the size of the canvas) abstract painting made this, its first appearance, at a time when Mondrian had not yet clipped its wings and schooled it (in 1916) to the geometrical and to discipline!

The painting was purchased by the State in 1949.

UDNIE

Picabia 1913

LOUIS VIVIN (1861–1936)
Notre-Dame de Paris

c. 1933, signed
Oil on canvas
Height 66 cm. (26″)
Width 81 cm. (32″)

Looking at this picture, one begins to understand why it was the Cubists and connoisseurs of Cubist painting who 'discovered' naïve or Neo-Primitive painting. It is at once the endorsement of Cubism and its antidote. Here, indeed, Vivin unconsciously applies two of the cardinal principles of Cubism: intellectual realism and the multiplying of angles of vision. Far from painting what he saw – the solid wall of the *quai*, for instance – he records each stone of which he knows the wall is built, and he is not afraid to show the façade and the side of the cathedral at once.

Continued on page 190

DOMINIQUE PEYRONNET (1872–1943)
Le Chateau de la Reine Blanche

1933, signed
Oil on canvas
Height 63 cm. (24³/₄″)
Width 81 cm. (32″)

This work is characteristic of naïve or Neo-Primitive painting in its precise drawing, its colour, which uses only local tones and encloses them within a strictly defined contour; in its handling, straightforward and careful in detail; and in its analytical vision and realism, in intention at least. But whilst pursuing minute realism, naïve painters succeed in achieving a decorative beauty and poetry too. Note the candour and purity with which the flower borders are here treated, recalling certain Gothic miniatures, and the general air of tranquillity. Salon des Indépendants, 1934 (No. 3522). Collection of Mme Grégory. Presented anonymously, 1948.

ANDRÉ BAUCHANT (1873–1958)   1945, signed and dated
LA FÊTE DE LA LIBÉRATION   Oil on canvas
                                                  Height 110 cm. (43¼")
                                                  Width 196 cm. (77")

Each of the 'twentieth-century primitives' preserves his originality, and develops his own particular domain for painting. Bauchant's is history. From ancient to modern times, it provides him with inspiration for scenes sacred or profane. As well as this picture, the Musée possesses *Louis XI faisant planter le mûrier en Touraine,* presented by the artist in 1950.

In *La Fête de la Libération* he is inspired by recent events – the Liberation of France in 1944. There have been few more moving tributes to this great episode in history, and despite certain clumsy elements peculiar to naïve painting, or perhaps even because of them, it has a truly epic and lyric quality. It brings to mind the work of Brueghel the Elder. The painting was presented anonymously in 1948.

FERNAND DESNOS (1901–1958)
LA CÈNE SUR LA SEINE

1954, signed and dated
Oil on canvas
Height 60 cm. (23¹/₂″)
Width 179 cm. (70¹/₂″)

Desnos was a concièrge in Paris and, like Caillaud, Vivancos and Van-
dersteen, belonged to the second wave of 'primitives' to come into the
public eye, following on the wave that took in Vivin, Bauchant, Bombois,
Peyronnet and others. His painting has the same characteristics as theirs,
technically and also in its essence, and the same flavour; that is, it is in
the popular taste and at the same time truly poetic. What an extraordinary
notion this is – suggested, it seems, by a rather trivial pun – to set Christ
and his Disciples for the Last Supper on the footway of the Pont des Arts
and group round them a little crowd of people thick with various celebrities,
whose faces were familiar to the painter from political, sports, theatre and
other pages of the Press! This bringing together of unlikely elements – like
the sofa and the virgin forest in the Douanier Rousseau's *Dream of
Yadwigha* – creates a surprising poetry, so much the more moving since it
is accompanied by a genuinely religious note. The painting of the sky,
luminous and clear like those of Vivin, the decorative effect of the trees
on the Ile de la Cité, the treatment of the houses on the right, their sharp
outline and the piquant colour recalling Utrillo, may be enjoyed in their
own right.
    Presented by the Société des Amis du Musée National d'Art Moderne, 1959.

SÉRAPHINE, real name Séraphine Louis (1864–1934) c. 1929, signed
THE TREE OF PARADISE Oil on canvas
Height 195 cm. (76³/₄")
Width 129 cm. (50³/₄")

The German artist W. Uhde, a leading connoisseur of Cubist and Neo-Primitive painting, was spending a holiday at Senlis in 1912 when he found to his astonishment that Séraphine, the servant he was employing during this summer stay, was a painter, and practised her art with uncommon success. Uhde encouraged her in her painting until the onset of madness put an end to it. Séraphine is a visionary artist rather than a 'naïve' painter – there is no trace here of the characteristic qualities of the 'twentieth-century primitives', such as precise draughtsmanship, a studied handling, analytical vision and attention to reality. She deals with one theme only – plant life, – and flings on to her canvas astonishing bouquets, extraordinary flowering shrubs, where the leaves end in feathers and where flower petals have wide-open eyes. The glow of the colour, bearing no relation to the tones of nature, and the furious sweep of the brush-work produce an hallucinatory effect. Beyond this, we note the splendour of the decorative detail, which equals that of oriental carpets or Chinese weaves, of which the simple servant-woman had in all likelihood never seen a single example. Purchased by W. Uhde from the artist. W. Uhde collection. Presented by Mlle A. M. Uhde in memory of Wilhelm Uhde, 1948.

Continued from page 186

Thus, unwittingly, he refutes those who denounce Cubism as being the product of a distorted intellectualism. Clearly, however, he puts Cubist formulas to work in a way very different from Braque's and Picasso's. What for the Cubists is the fruit of thought, method and will, for Vivin is the first draft – done from life. Hence the freshness of his work, all the more delectable as it is coupled with his exquisite gift for colour. Uhde Collection, 1948. Presented by Mlle A. M. Uhde in memory of her brother, 1948.

ANDRÉ DUNOYER DE SEGONZAC (born 1884)   1933, signed
BACCHUS   Oil on canvas
Height 66 cm. (26")
Width 92 cm. (36¼")
This Bacchus is, in fact, a sea-bather of the present day, bronzed by the
sun of Saint Tropez. The painter claims to follow tradition, yet here we
are far from Poussin, though fairly close to Courbet. Like him, Segonzac
has his roots in reality, and works by a set of principles which often follow
those of the Realists, who like to give first place to what is most concrete
in painting, the paint. Paint takes precedence over colour, shape and even
drawing. And yet, Segonzac's engravings, colour washes and water-colours
show a masterly skill in drawing. Here, the form of the work is massive;
density is given by the lavish application of pigment. This pigment, Segonzac's chief concern, renders excellently the muscular flesh, and the earth on
which the figure is solidly resting. Bought by the State.

JEAN-LOUIS BOUSSINGAULT (1883–1943)
WOMEN WITH GLADIOLI

Signed
Oil on canvas
Height 98 cm. (38½")
Width 165 cm. (65")

This is a decorative composition, a panel meant to form a pendant to the *Still life with basket of grapes*. The two canvases are splendid pieces of work and typical examples of this painter's art. The only criticism of them might be that, although intended to go together, they do not really balance one another: the forms in the two paintings are not on the same scale. However, *Women with gladioli* shows Boussingault painting with a force worthy of Courbet. What density and power there is, and reality too, in the fleshy, living arm of the figure on the left! And note the figure on the right – how the curving breast like some ripening fruit positively glows. Boussingault in this picture gives the first hint of the genius for colour that flowered so brilliantly towards the end of his career. Here in the bouquet of gladiolus, the most varied tones are sumptuously blended. Retrospective Exhibition at the Musée des Arts Décoratifs, 1944 (No. 2). Presented by Mme Abreu, 1948.

AMEDEO MODIGLIANI (1884–1920)　　　　　　　1917, signed
LOLOTTE　　　　　　　　　　　　　　　　　　　　Oil on canvas
　　　　　　　　　　　　　　　　　　　　　　Height 58 cm. (23")
　　　　　　　　　　　　　　　　　　　　Width 35 cm. (13³/₄")

The Musée d'Art Moderne prides itself on having two masterly sculptures by Modigliani, but it is poor in his canvases. A *Caryatid*, which was a sketch for one of his sculptures, comes as much from the hand of the sculptor as from that of the painter. His painting is only represented by this little head, which is not one of his best pictures. At any rate, it is a characteristic enough example of his work, as much because of its subject as of the execution. There is hardly a landscape or still-life in the whole output of Modigliani, which is almost wholly given up to portraying women. It is true there are portraits of men, such as those of Lipchitz, Soutine, and Cocteau, and of children, where he has perhaps done his very best work. However, while showing himself here and there to be strongly dominated by the influence of Cézanne, he is most himself in his nudes and portraits of women, which have also most appealed to the public in general. It may well be that he has expressed in them (like Ingres in similar subjects) the most obscure and individual strains in his personality: that sensuality, fined down and submitted to the intellect, at once cruel and tender, wholesome and morbid, straightforward and yet in love with the ideal, which gives so much enchantment to such works as the *Nude crouching*, and the portrait of Beatrice Hastings. In all these canvases the drawing prevails over the muted, sober colour, and over the form too, which is not expressed by the modelling but by the relation of the contours; it dominates even the rather thin and commonplace paint. It is by the line – long, flexible and sharp – that Modigliani expresses himself and expresses too the character of his model, elongating according to his own peculiar canon the line of the cheek, the oval of the chin and the contour of the full neck. In this he is honouring the tradition of draughtsmanship of his native Tuscany, and with it he combines influences from Negro art and from contemporary Cubism and Expressionism – all with such effortlessness and brio and, indeed, finesse, that his work has an indefinable magic, the secret and justification (with the great pathos of the artist's life) of his enormous success today.

CHAÏM SOUTINE (1894–1944)　　　　　　c. 1927, signed
THE PAGE-BOY　　　　　　　　　　　　Oil on canvas
　　　　　　　　　　　　　　　　Height 98 cm. (38^1/$_2$")
　　　　　　　　　　　　　　　　Width 80 cm. (31^1/$_2$")

This picture, painted 1927–1928, and *The Chasseur* of the Rothschild
Collection are the finest examples of a series in the artist's happiest vein.
The nervous and incisive line is used to good effect to harden the contours
and to set off the lobe from the rest of the ear, chin from cheek, shoulder
from collar-bone, giving the outline the disjointed look that can be seen,
though with less exaggeration, in some German masters of the late Middle
Ages. The figure, here drawn out, there contracted, shows a complete disregard for anatomy; Soutine is concerned to stress the underlying character
of the puny and ailing body of his model and to communicate his poignant
sympathy for this child condemned so early to labour. However, this
portrait – dashed off with a fevered brush – is not just so much pain,
suffering and despair, for Soutine's art enables him to exalt the wretchedness. He does this first by colour, choosing red, enhanced by a background
of steely blue, cold and sombre; red which evokes blood and fire, but has
also a certain gaudy splendour; but even more, by presenting the page-
boy direct and full-face. Following a method favoured by Rouault, he puts
no detail, no intermediary plane, between the beholder and the figure
which seems to spring forth challengingly out of the very edges of the
canvas; the full-face pose also gives the figure a commanding scale, especially since it takes up the whole area of the canvas. The boy's attitude
– legs wide apart, hands on hips, arms akimbo, and even more, the deliberate
elongation of left thigh, hands and arms, and the widening of the shoulders,
are all made to serve the design. Thus the sublime is one with suffering in
this portrait, very much as in the figure of Christ in fifteenth-century paintings. The picture carries a kind of religious emphasis as it becomes in some
sense the poem of exploited and suffering childhood. Happily there is
nothing literary in all this: it is solely by plastic means that Soutine makes
his appeal and, more than anything else, by that vast splash of plain blood-
red, its radiance increased by the splendour of the pigment.

　　Formerly in the Matsukata Collection, confiscated in 1944. Became the
property of the French State in 1952, under the terms of the Peace Treaty
with Japan.

AMÉDÉE DE LA PATELLIÈRE (1890–1932)   1929, signed
THE END OF THE WORLD   Oil on cardboard
Height 73 cm. (28³/₄″)
Width 92 cm. (36¹/₄″)

This apocalyptic composition is dated 1929, a year when the artist painted his most visionary canvases. A perspective recalling the poetic ones of Chirico serves as a framework for these 'extraordinary' objects so much favoured by the Surrealists – a column, a sphere, two skulls, two horses. And the fantastic is conjured up not so much by their assembling, or by the floating book at which the phantom points, as by the lunar chiaroscuro that envelops the whole canvas, the light cast by the black moon, and the feeling with which the painter has conceived the objects and animals in the composition.

Retrospective La Patellière Exhibition, Musée National d'Art Moderne, 1948. Purchased from Mme de La Patellière by the Musées Nationaux, 1947.

MARCEL GROMAIRE (born 1892)   1939, signed and dated
THE VAGABOND   Oil on canvas
Height 100 cm. (39¹/₂")
Width 81 cm. (32")

Gromaire always denied that he was an Expressionist. All the same, it is difficult, in face of this picture, to endorse his opinion. Expressionism may be held to consist in a subjective interpretation of reality, in an exaggerated statement of the experience of the painter, who seeks in this way to communicate it to us all the more forcibly; also in the use of a series of distortions meant, taken as a whole, to make us feel what the artist has felt and penetrate the inherent nature and inner mystery of a scene. If this

199

MARCEL GROMAIRE (born 1892) 1935, signed and dated
THE LINES OF THE HAND Oil on canvas
Height 100 cm. (39^1/$_2$")
Width 81 cm. (32")

Marcel Gromaire was a man of the North and in spirit quite akin to the leading Belgian Expressionists, especially Gustave de Smet and Brusselmans, though the compelling structure of the figures in this canvas, their simplified contour, the muted colour, and the way they are put together according to an obvious governing plan, owe much to Cubism – and to Cézanne's Cubism. Expressionist features in Gromaire's work are his concern with a theme animated by figures – more broadly human than the still-lifes of such absorbing interest to Braque and Picasso, – an intention to be more immediately understood through an art that does less transposing of reality, and the almost caricatured treatment of the faces, which takes less heed of the plastic problems than a desire to stress exactly what they are. Other features place him at some distance from Expressionism, such as a constant concern with the decorative and mural quality, purposed nobility of style, the exercise of powers of reflexion and will – all these account for his future development, that took him towards his success in tapestry design-ing. The painting was purchased by the State in 1936.

Continued from page 199

is a true description, then this striking *Vagabond* is indeed Expressionist. Gromaire has turned this mortal, flesh-and-blood creature into a statue of wood – an iron-hard wood likely to resist the ravages of time. He stresses all that declares the crude violence of the character by distorting certain details of his body and his clothes. The folds of his shirt become steel-barbed, his mouth a knife-blade, his nose a wedge that could cleave a tree trunk; the chin is squared and the fist enlarged to be of more consequence than the head – all indicating that his mental life was less developed than the physical. But (and here Gromaire's claim is warranted) his Expression-ism never asserts itself at the expense of the very strict modelling. The artist in no wise neglects drawing, colour, form, composition, paint or execution, and in that way is successful in giving form to his ideas and his feelings. The painting was purchased by the State.

EDOUARD GOERG (born 1893)   1929, signed
THE PRETTY FLOWER-GIRL   Oil on canvas
Height 80 cm. (31¹/₂″)
Width 65 cm. (25¹/₂″)

Goerg is one of the most typical representatives of Expressionism as it developed in Paris between the two World Wars. This phase of the movement, the sequel of that introduced by Rouault in 1902, is related to the Expressionism that swept through Europe at that time, taking hold conspicuously in Germany, where it was always most at home, being an art form well suited to the native genius; the connection between the work of Goerg and that of German painters such as George Grosz or Otto Dix of the years 1925–1930 is very close. The Flemish Expressionism of Permeke, Gustave de Smet and Brusselmans, for instance, has a distinctly popular strain and is often quite peasant in character. In Goerg, as in the Germans, on the other hand, we find the disillusionment of the urban man and the morbid outlook of an over-refined intellectual – features that make for a most subtle and uncommon variation of Expressionism. It is the triumph of a taste for ugliness and caricature, sarcastic comment, of a pessimistic view of the world, of outrageous distortion, dark and unusual chromatism, and a chiaroscuro intended to emphasize the extraordinary character of the scene represented. But Goerg takes a different path from his German rivals: his penetration of character is not so emphatic, his accent is less harsh; there is less political partisanship, and he is far more taken up with realizing his concept as a painting. All these factors can easily be discerned here. The beauty of the very elaborate and thick-laid pigment, the density of the warm and velvety blacks, the subtle harmonies of the tones – these provide a counterbalance to the clear-cut delineation of the character and the almost malignant glint in the expression. So this painting carries a hint of Goerg's future work – the taste for rich and uncommon tones, shimmering pigment, for merging shapes, and a strange and fantastic kind of beauty that was a feature of his art particularly just after the Second World War. *Les Egoutiers* in the Musée d'Art Moderne is a good example of this later manner of Goerg, less Expressionist perhaps, or Expressionist in a different way. Presented by M. Paul Guillaume in 1933.

FRANÇOIS DESNOYER (born 1894)
ESCALES

1940, signed
Oil on canvas
Height 180 cm. (71")
Width 220 cm. (86½")

Among the painters of the inter-war period, Desnoyer has a rather special place. He gave much more thought than Gromaire or Goerg to the lessons of the earlier *avant-garde* movements, particularly Fauvism and Cubism, but he interpreted them in the spirit of Expressionism, which inspired a good number of other painters of the period. It is clear what the construction, in its sharp definition and geometric design, owes to Cézanne and Cubism. The colour has an uncouth violence that harks back to the Fauves. Desnoyer remains, too, in the stream of all contemporary painting since Cézanne, Seurat and Gauguin, as can be seen by the care he takes to fill the whole of the canvas with shapes, leaving no uncovered area; to raise the horizon; to ignore perspective by hanging behind the figures a backcloth of houses and the surrounding scene; to press the individuals into a very mannered grouping and to sharpen the lines of force of the composition.

But all these expedients are at the service of Desnoyer's ardent and driving search to get at character – of the individuals, women, sailors, musicians, and especially of the city, this great port of Marseilles that he portrays so successfully with its swarming crowds and raffish poetry.

In the Salon des Indépendants, 1940 (No. 393). Purchased by the State from the artist.

CHARLES WALCH (1898–1948)　　　　　　　　1939, signed
THE BLUE WINDOW　　　　　　　　　　　　　Oil on canvas
　　　　　　　　　　　　　　　　　　　　Height 65 cm. (25¹/₂″)
　　　　　　　　　　　　　　　　　　　　Width 59 cm. (23¹/₄″)

In Charles Walch we have a poet, a delightful magician who conjures up a dream-world peopled with women and children, field flowers and familiar animals, companionable things and radiant sunlight. These details that recur in his pictures he sometimes places in smiling landscapes – perhaps under snow, – at other times in quiet interiors conveying their serene homeliness with great felicity. Indeed, these scenes are conceived in a full flight of imagination: the bouquets of flowers are given a larger scale than the people because Walch takes more delight in exaggerating the glowing flowers than in portraying the figures. The painter knows no laws other than those of his heart and his joy – yet he never forgets the rules of painting and faithfully observes them. First covering his canvas with colours and concerned only to make them all harmonize, he then gives substance to those tones that will become here a dress, there a tree or even a ball of wool. In this way Walch achieves the most delicate precision in the polychrome mottling, reflecting his Alsatian taste – so steeped is he in the traditional art of his native province. His pigment, melting, shimmering, reveals the same homely devotion to the fine craftsmanship of Alsace. And since these dreams of Walch are so perfectly realised in terms of painting, they have all the greater force of conviction, and overwhelming charm.

The painting was presented anonymously in 1950.

MARC CHAGALL (born 1887)
A LA RUSSIE, AUX ÂNES ET AUX AUTRES

1911, signed and dated
Oil on canvas
Height 156 cm. (61¹/₂″)
Width 122 cm. (48″)

Chagall arrived in Paris from Russia in 1911 and got in touch with Cubist circles. He also made contact with the Expressionists in Germany, where Walden, director of *Der Sturm* Gallery in Berlin, welcomed him with open arms. The various influences he came under were fused with his earliest style of the years before 1914 to produce a synthesis that was wholly his own.

From Cubism he took the very precise structure of form, the firm contour and the compelling evidence of the composition; from German Expressionism he adopted vivid and heavy colour that scorns any semblance of reality. From Russian peasant art he inherited a blithe medley of tones and many elements of folklore. All was made to serve an imagination filled with fantasy, to which he gave free rein, thus anticipating the Surrealists. Indeed it can be said that Chagall, in company with Chirico, more surely than any other painters on the eve of the 1914 War, pointed the way to Surrealism.

In the Chagall Exhibition, Musée National d'Art Moderne, Paris, 1947 (No. 9). Presented by the artist in 1949.

1917, signed and dated
Oil on canvas
Height 233 cm. (91³/₄")
Width 136 cm. (53¹/₂")

Not many works could better illustrate Chagall's art than this, and for several reasons. First, it is a portrait of the painter himself. In the second place, it also portrays the features of Bella Chagall, his wife and inspiration, whom he often painted in the years following 1909 until her death in 1944. Third, this dual portrait is a characteristic expression of a vein of inspiration often worked by Chagall: almost every year, on the anniversary of his marriage, he would do a commemorative painting. This particular dual portrait moreover, (and here is a fourth reason), includes a landscape – a Russian landscape in fact. This genre accounts for some of Chagall's happiest achievements. Clearly, too, the influence of his native Russia was a vital element in his work.

This canvas was painted in 1917 when the artist was back in Vitebsk after some years in the army; the view of the town shows the hold the Russian scene had on him. Not that he reproduces it at all slavishly: the claims of fantasy are never denied. Here, Chagall's head is not an extension of the neck, and it has a kind of angel floating above it; he is seen astride the shoulders of his wife who, a fan in her hand, is treading the waters of a river as serenely as a meadow or a carpet. This painter-poet is not much concerned with the probable. At the same time, there is a substratum of the traditional in all Chagall's painting, and it derives in part from its links with a folklore common to all countries and shared by all traditional arts. J. J. Sweeney, in his work on Chagall, has reproduced, alongside this *Double portrait*, an English inn sign attributed to Hogarth: this shows a woman holding a glass of wine and sitting astride a man on a village green; the resemblance is obvious. Certainly Chagall has his share of a distinct kind of humour and a particular aesthetic which, in every country, are the attributes of artists working in the traditional spirit. His part, however, has an originality that this kinship even enhances. Not only does fantasy, with him, prevail over irony, but forms tend to be disembodied and throw off the bondage of weight. Further, the diminutive scale of the landscape and its humble role, the elongation of the figures, which appear all the larger by contrast, their arrangement in a spiral and the swirling effect thus given to them (as to certain figures of El Greco) – all these elements tend to make unearthly beings of these figures, possessed of the power of levitation, beings of pure spirit who rise like the spiral curl of a

MARC CHAGALL (born 1887)
<small>AUTOUR D'ELLE</small>

1945, signed and dated
Oil on canvas
Height 131 cm. (51¹/₂″)
Width 109 cm. (43″)

This picture was painted by Chagall as a tribute to his first wife Bella, who had died in the previous year. He has grouped about the well-loved figure various objects which his memory clung to. In the centre is an apparition of the Russian city of Smolensk, where he had married Bella in 1915; on the upper right hand, a married couple; on the left, the painter himself, palette in hand, close to the canvas being painted. He is in thrall to his fantasy, and is driven to evoke strange shapes. Himself he paints with head upside down; a bird with a hand holds a candlestick; in the centre he places one of those attenuated fine-spun angels that he especially affects. The whole scene is thus steeped in an atmosphere of the fantastic, intensified by the choice of colours and the handling of the shapes which, lacking any substance, seem like astral bodies. In the colours the blues dominate, dark and limpid, and to their range are added strange violets and some greens. Thus we get an impression of something ethereal and nocturnal – the impression of a dream, the dream pursued by Chagall, brush in hand, whilst he dwells upon the figure in whose honour he has painted this poetic canvas.

Chagall Exhibition, Musée National d'Art Moderne, Paris, 1947 (No. 61). Presented by the artist, 1949.

Continued from page 210

flame towards an empyrean where an angel awaits them. Chagall's dream of disembodiment has rarely been more successfully translated than in this canvas, in which traditional comedy and fantasy adorn the dream with good humour, grace and mischief.

Chagall Exhibition, Musée d'Art Moderne, 1947 (No. 21). Presented by the artist, 1947.

212

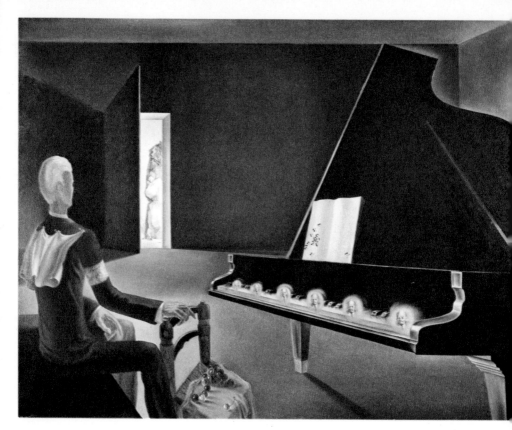

SALVADOR DALI (born 1904)
COMPOSITION

1931, signed and dated
Oil on canvas
Height 114 cm. (45″)
Width 146 cm. (57¹/₂″)

This is a picture characteristic of the Surrealism of about 1930. The surrealist painter wholly gives himself up to transcribing his visions or nightmares without worry about their strangeness or incoherence. In this canvas, as in dreams, the automatic and free association of ideas is the governing principle: it is easy to grasp the connection that turns the red cross on a medical orderly's arm-band into red cherries, and the notes of music into ants. The imagination of the Surrealists is rarely as exuberant as that of Klee or Chagall or Redon, and their art is far more conventional. To prove to us, in fact, that in their pictures the plastic expression is of less importance than the evidence on the nature of human personality, they like to adopt a strictly academic technique. Purchased by the State.

JOAN MIRÓ (born 1893)　　　　　　　　1945, signed and dated
THE BULL-FIGHT　　　　　　　　　　　　　　　Oil on canvas
　　　　　　　　　　　　　　　　　　　　Height 114 cm. (45″)
　　　　　　　　　　　　　　　　　　　Width 144 cm. (56³/₄″)

Joan Miró, the Catalan, was not a very orthodox Surrealist; he took from
Surrealism hardly more than an inclination to fantasy. His art bears the
mark of the search for a new pictorial expression quite unknown in
Tanguy and Dali. Perspective, modelling, chiaroscuro, over-polished paint
and painstaking finish he rejects. In a world of two dimensions he puts
in figures of which the drawing owes much to the prehistoric rock engravings of Eastern Spain. The colouring, too, is often borrowed from the
traditional art of the Balearic Isles. The paint is laid on sparsely, the
handling is nimble and witty, and a subtle note of humour always lights
up the work of Miró, a fine craftsman and poet. The canvas was presented
by the artist in 1947.

MAX ERNST (born 1891)
APRÈS MOI, LE SOMMEIL

1958, signed and dated
Oil on canvas
Height 130 cm. (51")
Width 89 cm. (35")

Max Ernst, like Miró, is a Surrealist who very often breaks away from the academic technique laid down by the movement. Certainly some of his works, especially round about 1920–25, show a handling of a most traditional and conventional kind – no doubt the effect of the spirit of disparagement, derision and all-round scepticism that had already swayed him during his Dadaist period. About 1926–28, however, he began to take the prescriptions and taboos of Surrealism rather casually and gave himself up to his deep-seated liking for independence and poetry. Thus he came to create a fantastic and disturbing world, which finds its most characteristic expression in the landscapes of hallucination he painted about 1940 (with *La Nuit Rhénane* of 1945). Later on, the disturbing aspect of his work is toned down, but the fantastic remains, becoming progressively lighter, more ethereal and delicate. This is the manner of *Après moi, le sommeil*. It is dedicated to Paul Eluard, for whom Ernst had always felt such a lively admiration that he broke with the Surrealist group in 1938, when they ordered their followers to sabotage the poetry of Paul Eluard by all possible means.

The drawing, precise and sharp, possesses nevertheless an extreme lightness. The colour brings out the same fine sensitivity as most of the other contemporary canvases of Max Ernst: subtle greys, pinkish whites and blues delicately faded, go to make a crystal and exquisite harmony. The paint appears diaphanous and the brush-work almost caressing. Something indefinably winged and ethereal seems to pass into the visions held fast by Ernst on the canvas. In this respect he is the heir of what was best in the German Romantic movement and perpetuates the spirit of his great fellow-countrymen Novalis, Heine and Schumann.

In the Max Ernst Exhibition, Musée National d'Art Moderne, 1959 (No. 90). Presented by the artist, 1960.

ANDRÉ MASSON (born 1896) 1932
L'ENLÈVEMENT Oil on canvas
Height 137 cm. (53¹/₂″)
Width 116 cm. (45¹/₂″)

Generally, André Masson is placed amongst the Surrealists, and he has indeed exhibited with them. But there is hardly any relation between the greater part of his work and such wholly Surrealist manifestations as the *Evocation of Lenin* of Dali or the *Palais aux rochers de fenêtres* of Tanguy – to take only two examples, both from the Musée d'Art Moderne. Unlike these painters, indeed, Masson most often seems (and especially in this *Enlèvement)* less concerned to express his inner visions and explore the mysteries of creation than to concentrate on the problems of painting – problems of colour and, even more, of rhythm. In this picture there seems hardly any doubt that he has borrowed the general arrangement from the *Abduction of the Daughters of Leucippus* by Rubens (Munich Pinakothek). However, in doing this he creates an entirely different work, at once more vividly descriptive and the product of deeper thought. In the picture in the Musée d'Art Moderne we find no trace of that delight in the paint, transparent and silky, which we see in the Flemish master's canvas. There is no pearly light here, nor yet the fleshy forms of Rubens' picture, and nothing recalls his sensual feeling for life. Masson's painting is more intellectual, further removed from actuality, and his sole aim has been to make a pattern of arabesques and splashes of colour, all the more severe for the pigment being thin and the handling more astringent to the eye. But for all that, the calligraphy and the chromatism are proof of great flexibility and mastery. Thanks to these qualities this study in painting attains the status of an achieved work of art on its own terms.

The painting was presented by M. Rosenberg in 1946.

LE CORBUSIER, real name Edouard Jeanneret (born 1887)

STILL-LIFE   1922, signed and dated
Oil on canvas
Height 65 cm. (25¹/₂")
Width 81 cm. (31¹/₂")

World-famous as an architect under the name Le Corbusier, Jeanneret first appeared in the world of art as a painter. With Ozenfant, he was the founder in 1920 of Purism. This picture is a good example of the Purist aesthetic. Subject is a matter of indifference, the drawing is exact and even more severe than that of the Cubists. The colour is sober and leaden, but has great subtlety. Shapes are clear, sharp and forceful, the composition all the clearer for being built up on a single plane. The artist is possessed by a sublime asceticism. Still, there is no lack of poetry – sober and low-pitched, as in so many still-lifes by seventeenth-century French painters.

Salon des Indépendants, 1923 (No. 2419). Presented by the artist, 1955.

WASSILI KANDINSKY (1866–1944)
DÉVELOPPEMENT EN BRUN

1933, signed and dated
Oil on canvas
Height 100 cm. (39¹/₂″)
Width 120 cm. (47¹/₄″)

Kandinsky was born in Russia but worked chiefly in Germany. With the coming of Nazism he sought refuge at Neuilly-sur-Seine in 1933. But an earlier visit to France in 1905–1906 was decisive in his development, as the impact of contemporary French painting, Fauvism especially, set his course towards a highly-coloured Expressionism, from which he made the easy passage into abstract art. This canvas, painted in Berlin in August 1930, was the last he did in Germany and the last in the severe style he had used since 1922, under the influence of the *Bauhaus*. By contrast with the lyric fire which had lit up his abstract works of the Munich und Moscow

WASSILI KANDINSKY (1866–1944)
AMBIGUITY, COMPLEX – SIMPLE

1939, signed and dated
Oil on canvas
Height 100 cm. (39½″)
Width 81 cm. (32″)

This picture, which is no. 477 in Kandinsky's own catalogue of his works, is deservedly one of his most famous canvases. The drawing shows extreme liveliness and sensibility, the colour is light and piquant, proof of unfailing taste and subtlety. We have a new element in Kandinsky – the painting is saturated with pearly light, different both from the light in his work at Murnau and Munich, which is heavy and hard, and from the semi-abstract light (transparency rather than light) in the canvases of his Dessau period. The paint that holds this light makes one think of satin or an Oriental lacquer. Still, this rather forced, mannered quality does not detract from the noble grace of a composition based on the contrast between the straight lines upper left and the curves lower right; between the tapered oval masses in the lower left and those, circular and spread out in wide bulges, in the other corner. Thus, around the two concentric circles, the shapes balance one another in a skilful counterpoint, and the dignity of the design complements the delicacy of colour, light and pigment. The imagination that plays over this blending of wholly different qualities seems to have its origin in remotest Asia, and to flower here in the genial air of the Ile de France. An indefinable breath of China or Japan (the horizontals and verticals in the upper left make a design reminiscent of Torri) blends with a light almost Impressionist in its brilliance, giving an extraordinary poetry and even, one might say, the gleam of a smile – a serenity that never lit up Kandinsky's work before he came to live at Neuilly. Presented by the Société des Amis du Musée d'Art Moderne, 1958.

Continued from page 221

period of 1910–1923, this picture derives from an art informed by the will, disciplined, austere, with colours and paint used sparingly, the brush-work deliberate, the shapes and composition severe, and the drawing geometric in concept – an art that is a little dry, almost attenuated, rather doctrinaire and academic, noble, impressive, splendid in its breadth, confidence and authority. It is this work that Grohmann compared to a 'funeral march' in its low-pitched and extremely rhythmic arrangement of planes, painted 'in solemn tones of brown'. Bought by the Musées Nationaux, 1959.

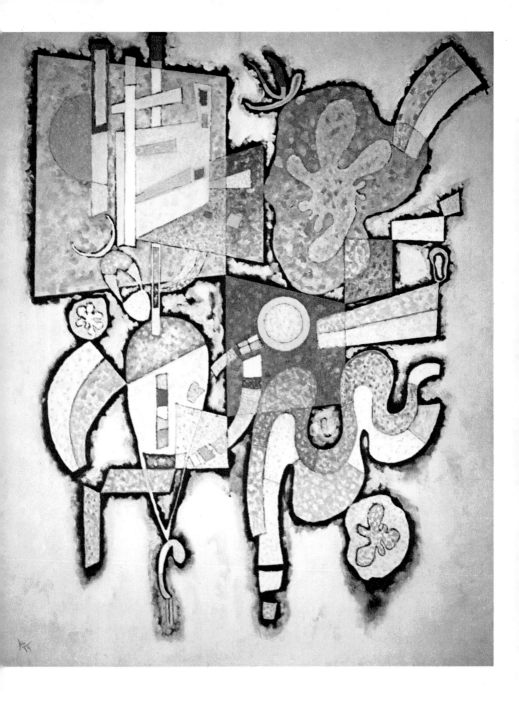

ALBERTO MAGNELLI (born 1888) 1937, signed and dated
RONDE OCÉANIQUE Oil on canvas
Height 114 cm. (45″)
Width 146 cm. (57½″)

Italy turned to abstract painting not long after France, Germany and
Russia. Some of the Futurists drifted into it round about 1914, and
towards 1916 Magnelli, a young painter from Tuscany, took the same
course. In 1930 he left Italy for France. The wind was set for strict abstraction, and *Ronde océanique* has severe draughtmanship and a sober
colour-scale. But this severity does not mean dryness: the execution, sweeping and sensitive, and the full rhythm, make a vigorous and concentrated
life flow into it. They add, too, a solemn note of music to the precision of
this studied composition. Purchased by the State from the artist in 1950.

ANTOINE PEVSNER (born 1886)   1944–1948, signed and dated
Spatial picture   Oil on wood panel
Height 81 cm. (32″)
Width 100 cm. (39¹/₂″)

Antoine Pevsner is not only one of the most distinguished *avant-garde* sculptors of our century, he has also a considerable amount of work to his credit as a painter. It was in painting that in 1911–1912 he began producing his first abstract works. Passing on to sculpture, he still did not forsake his first medium. *Spatial picture* has a close relation to his sculpture: there is the same precision due to geometric lines that are simple but nevertheless have feeling; the same rigorous structure of the volumes and care in the execution. The colour has a purity and a limpid quality of the same order as Pevsner achieves in the bronze, copper and brass he uses in his sculpture. A. Pevsner Exhibition, Musée National d'Art Moderne 1956–57 (No. 15). Purchased by the Musées Nationaux from the artist, 1957.

ROGER BISSIÈRE (born 1888)
COMPOSITION AUX TONALITÉS VERTES

1955, signed and dated
Oil on canvas
Height 130 cm. (51″)
Width 152 cm. (60″)

Bissière, like Jacques Villon, was late in finding himself as a painter. In sympathy with Purism and on the fringes of Cubism, he is one of the few painters of the generation after the Cubists who, between the two Wars, supported the claims of pure painting and *avant-garde* art. It was especially after 1945 that his genius took wing. The sparkle, luminosity and transparency of his colour are seen to good effect in this painting. A true craftsman, he achieves more and more lightness as his handling broadens. Abstract or figurative? The question hardly arises, so brimming is his work with life, pictorial quality and poetry. Bissière Exhibition, Galerie Jeanne Bucher, 1956. Purchased by the State, 1956.

ROGER BISSIÈRE (born 1888)   1925, signed and dated
LANDSCAPE   Oil on wood panel
Height 135 cm. (53″)
Width 85 cm. (33¹/₂″)

Among the paintings which Bissière gave to the Musée d'Art Moderne
he included, in 1959, this early canvas, in spite of his extreme, even
excessive, severity towards all his work prior to 1937. He chose it, clearly,
because he considered it had an especial quality – and justifiably. This
canvas is 'Cézannian', but it already gives proof of such an originality
that there is no great gap between this figurative work and the abstract
pictures Bissière was to paint from 1945–48 onwards. It often happens

ANDRÉ BEAUDIN (born 1895)
LE POIDS DE L'EAU

1954, signed and dated
Oil on canvas
Height 162 cm. (63³/₄")
Width 130 cm. (51")

Like Pignon and André Marchand, Beaudin is one of those artists who reject abstraction and yet transform to the utmost the reality that provides their inspiration and which they cannot forego. However, he himself effects this transposition by a method indebted far more than theirs to Cubism.

It is true the chromatism, fairly vivid despite the greys, gets away from the colour most favoured by the Cubists. Yet we recall just those painters, and Gris in particular, as we notice the precise drawing, considered and carefully balanced composition, the economy in the paint, and the deliberately impersonal execution. Nevertheless there is no lack of feeling and poetry, and they are so much the more convincing since his great restraint keeps them obscure.

Salon de Mai, 1956 (No. 13). Purchased by M. Georges Salles. Selected by the French Jury for the Prix Guggenheim (1956). Prix Guggenheim Exhibition, Musée National d'Art Moderne, 1956. Guggenheim Museum, New York, 1957. Presented by M. Salles, 1956.

Continued from page 227

that an artist gives an indication in his early works of what he will go on to accomplish in his mature years, even in his old age, at the climax of a long career maybe in quite other fields of experiment. This is the case with Bissière who, in this canvas, uses a colour range, gets the effect of light, employs a handling and arrives at a pigment, that are all pointers to the features that distinguish the splendid flowering of his painting during the last fifteen years or so. This work of his youth, besides its prophetic quality, possesses a further interest: it shows how frail, indeed even arbitrary, the frontier is between the abstract and the figurative. As a landscape this picture has the appearance, at a glance, of being only quasi-abstract, like many of the painter's abstract compositions, which are so instinct with vitality and truth that they seem to be portraits (which in fact they are) of the hidden and inherent forces of nature.

CHARLES LAPICQUE (born 1898)   1950, signed and dated
PORTRAIT OF THE DUC DE NEMOURS   Oil on canvas
Height 195 cm. (76³/₄″)
Width 97 cm. (38″)

Lapicque was interested in the constant change in art forms and, to his
credit, never tied himself to any particular style. He anticipated the
experiments that his younger friends, Bazaine, Estève, Manessier and
others, made before and after the Second World War. But he did not
travel their path, making instead a definite return towards the figurative. The portrait of the Duc de Nemours is one of a set of compositions

Continued on page 232

EDOUARD PIGNON (born 1905)
The Pink Sail

1948, signed and dated
Oil on canvas
Height 130 cm. (51")
Width 195 cm. (76³/₄")

Pignon, after having used a style full of colour in which the structure of
the volumes is stated with a robust sturdiness, drifted about 1948 towards
one that is more flexible and more subdued in its colour-scale. This may
have come about under the influence of the light of Ostend, where he was
staying when he painted this picture. Greys and pinks predominate, and
their lightness harmonizes well with the fluid, very thin quality of the
paint and the swift ease of the execution. There is the same flexibility in
the composition, built up on obliques and ellipses, in which elegance and
the dynamic are fused. Their evident simplicity also gives the canvas
a severity and dignity, emphasized by the simplifying of the shapes and
the layout of the tones in big, unbroken expanses. Thus we find the sense
of life at one with structural grandeur. The painting was purchased by the
State from the artist.

ANDRÉ MARCHAND (born 1907)
La Lumière de l'oiseau

1955, signed and dated
Oil on canvas
Height 195 cm. (76³/₄″)
Width 190 cm. (74³/₄″)

André Marchand was enthralled by the Camargue, its wild life, the marshes and the light. He painted many canvases of the region on the spot and an even greater number from his recollections. This mood explains the painting he has called *La lumière de l'oiseau*. He has introduced the flamingoes, so beautiful a feature of the region, and has successfully and audaciously interpreted the humid and dazzling light reflected in the pools and strands by a palette of blacks, greys and very dark earth-colours. This palette has yet other qualities, such as the accuracy, delicacy and elegant restraint that characterize the painting of the Far East. And it is again of the Far East one thinks in observing the precise draughtsmanship that gives definition to objects and allows them to stir, and at the same time is made up of rhythm and the arabesque. In this way Marchand achieves the decorative quality, and the feeling of music, while remaining anchored to reality and aware of his own inner life – an awareness he makes us share.

Salon de Mai, 1955 (No. 117). Marchand Exhibition, Galerie Charpentier, Paris, 1956 (98 c). Presented by the artist, 1960.

Continued from page 230

representing individuals in armour – generally of greater height than breadth – in which he nearly always takes up the whole canvas with a single figure. Stress on the vertical, together with the Gothic monumental, are thus characteristic of these works, and their origin may be found perhaps in the stained glass windows of French cathedrals. Lapicque turned away from the severity and simplicity of the contours he had favoured before 1945 and took to the elaborations of a curly line. He was a great admirer of Raoul Dufy and aligned himself with him in making line and colour not coincide. By this means he gets vibration, tremor and life, as well as decorative style. Bought by the State.

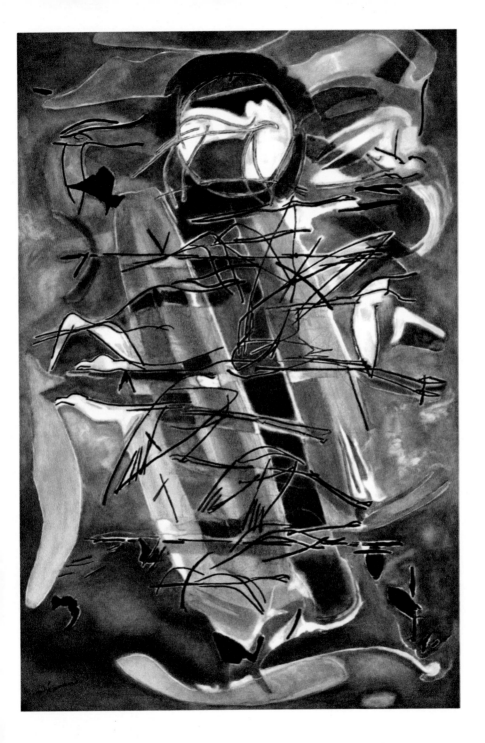

JEAN BAZAINE (born 1904)
Wind off the sea

1949, signed and dated
Oil on canvas
Height 119 cm. (46⁷/₈″)
Width 89 cm. (35″)

From about 1945 the forms in Bazaine's pictures are no longer recognizable. Even so, the painter always denied that he subscribed to abstract painting, against which, in fact, he wrote some closely argued pages in his first-rate *Notes d'un peintre*. Like Manessier, Singier, Le Moal, he derives from a different trend, one that might be called non-figurative. True, these painters cease to depict objects that can be identified, but for all that they are not withdrawn from the external world. The starting-point for the painter is always that of his contact with the world and it is often an equivalent of its realities that he means to set down on his canvas. He is a realist interpreter of underlying depths and a landscape painter of the hidden forces of nature, and when he adopts shapes that are no longer figurative he does so precisely the better to seize and express this boundless and unfathomable life of the world.

In this canvas, it is the wind off the sea that Bazaine has set out to paint. Hence, we have the composition based on a diagonal struck by bundles of horizontal parallels that correspond to the gusts of wind and the movement of the sea; hence also the palette of greenish blues and the blue-green violets that evoke the damp cold of the sea breeze rather than the colour of the waves, and the architectural structure, powerful and compelling, built up on lines that conflict and on precise rhythms, which give us the same impression as the force of the wind sweeping across space.

Presented by M. Bernard Maeght in 1954.

ALFRED MANESSIER (born 1911)　　　　　1950, signed and dated
THE CROWN OF THORNS　　　　　　　　　　　　Oil on canvas
　　　　　　　　　　　　　　　　　　　　　Height 163 cm. (64″)
　　　　　　　　　　　　　　　　　　　　　Width 98 cm. (38¹/₂″)

Manessier, like Bazaine and Singier, stands on the dividing line between the figurative and the abstract – or rather, that form of art where the figurative ceases to be recognizable, without actually becoming abstract. Evidence is provided by this painting, which derives from a vein of inspiration at once highly characteristic and one of his most original and successful – the religious motif. Manessier breaks (it goes without saying) not only with the 'Saint-Sulpice brand of pietism' by which Christian art of to-day is only too often debased, but also with the whole of a figurative tradition that illustrates and narrates sacred subjects. He conceives of religious painting as a meditation brush in hand, whose function is to induce the spectator to meditate in turn, and to prepare the way by enveloping him in a kind of contemplative and fervent atmosphere. In this canvas, Manessier has in mind the Passion of Christ and especially a specific episode: he sees the Crowning with Thorns as one of the agonies of Jesus but at the same time as the proclaiming, at the very instance of those who crowned him, of his sovereignty over the world. Suffering and majesty – these, then, are the two themes he means to suggest in this work, from which the figurative element is not entirely excluded: it is seen in a halo starred with spikes, which evokes rather than portrays the Crown of Thorns. The theme of suffering is conveyed by the dominant red with its suggestion of blood and by the interplay, insistent and rhythmic, of the parallel verticals, the bundle of rods which seems to associate the concept of the Crowning with the Flagellation. But this network of verticals, with their deliberate breaks, lifts the composition in a great soaring, even triumphal, movement. Although red is the colour of blood, it is also the Tyrian or Imperial purple. Thus the concept of the kingship of Christ emerges, and Manessier associates it by imperishable ties with that of the Passion.

Exhibition of Sacred Art, French Works of the 19th and 20th Centuries, Musée National d'Art Moderne, 1950 (Catalogue No. 86). Purchased from the artist by the State.

JEAN LE MOAL (born 1909)   1955, signed
FEAST OF ST JOHN, MIDSUMMER DAY   Oil on canvas
Height 116 cm. (45$^{1}/_{2}''$)
Width 89 cm. (38$^{1}/_{2}''$)

Le Moal, a friend of Manessier, followed the trend to the non-figurative
in painting. But it is with Singier and, above all, Bazaine rather than
Manessier (who was more drawn towards the spiritual) that he has affinity
– for like them he seeks to grasp the inner life of nature and to recreate
for us an all-embracing image of it in his compositions; these must, for
this to succeed, be non-figurative. Le Moal in this picture has been able

Continued on page 240

238

GUSTAVE SINGIER (born 1909) 1950, signed and dated
CHRISTMAS EVE Oil on canvas
Height 38 cm. (15″)
Width 46 cm. (18″)

Singier has painted very few religious works. All the same, how beautifully this painting comes off! We have the dark and limpid azure of the night sky aglow with soft and festive lights – the lanterns of the peasants going to midnight Mass, candles lighting up the church and the Christmas-trees, many hearth-fires, glint of stars that lift the heart with hope. Without representing anything at all, or rather *because* he does not represent anything, Singier succeeds in in suggesting everything – all that we associate with Christmas Eve. Exhibition of Sacred Art, French Works of the 19th and 20th Centuries, Musée National d'Art Moderne, 1950 (No. 124). Purchased from the artist by the State.

MARIE HÉLÈNE VIEIRA DA SILVA (born 1908)

HANGING GARDENS　　　　　　　　　　　　　1955, signed and dated
Oil on canvas
Height 165 cm. (65″)
Width 113 cm. (44¹/₂″)

As an instance of the difficulty of drawing the line between abstract and figurative painting, and the point at which the dispute between their champions becomes fatuous, we have only to go to the work of Marie Hélène Vieira da Silva – one among many examples. She is Portuguese in origin but settled in France in 1928, where she became naturalized in 1956. Whether she still clings to representation of objects in this picture and still holds the mirror up to nature, it would need a very acute critic to determine – one as penetrating as Mme da Silva herself, whose art is all grace, delicacy and fastidiousness. The light and sharply-incised drawing brings to mind the well-known remark on Joubert – done 'with the quill of an angel'. On the white background, snowy, silvery white, delicate accents of blues and ochres stand out. The shapes, filmy and weightless, quiver in the light. Nor does the balance of the composition weight it in any way: this severe arrangement as a whole appears frail, about to break up as the elements composing it take wing. The paint is no more than a film and the execution is done by the lightest of hands. The vigour and firm assurance do nothing to detract from its ethereal character. Here Mme da Silva reconciles opposites, just as she reconciles rigorous modelling with fluidity and poetry. She shows us a world of the imagination and fantasy, gardens of Faërie, inviting us to forget everything and yield ourselves up to the delight of their beauty. Purchased from the artist by the State, 1956.

Continued from page 238

to express the full force of summer bursting into flower. The dynamic quality of the painting, the radiance of the colour, in which reds and blues predominate (reds evoking the heat and blues the light), the limpid paint suggesting the clear air – all these means are used here to celebrate the idea of summer at its height. Purchased by the State in 1956.

MAURICE ESTÈVE (born 1904)
REBECCA

1952, signed and dated
Oil on canvas
Height 92 cm. (36¼″)
Width 73 cm. (28¾″)

Estève, more abstract than Bazaine, is wholly given up to covering his canvas with lines, shapes and radiant and expressive colours. With that done and the painting finished, he gives it a title that has the same kind of significance as the distinguishing name of a sonata. He is a subtle colourist, certainly outstripping anyone of his generation, and he is unmatched in the way he brings together, as here, purples and golds, violets and vermilions, pinks and greens, lemon yellows and blues, which he harmonizes with blacks. His handling is equally skilful. The pigment, rich and thick and yet not heavy, catches the light and shimmers; at the same time it shows that superlative craftsmanship, the mark of the French School, without which, if we think of Fouquet, Georges de La Tour, Chardin, Corot, Cézanne, Seurat, Rouault, Braque, the picture would be a failure, abortive, unsatisfying – in a word, potential rather than accomplished. For it is not ideas that make a painting, but the painter's use of his materials, and the most profound philosophy will never produce anything but bad painting unless it becomes one with the life of the picture.

In the Salon des Tuileries, 1952 (No. 73). Purchased from the artist by the State.

HANS HARTUNG (born 1904)
Painting T 54 – 16

1954, signed and dated
Oil on canvas
Height 130 cm. (51")
Width 97 cm. (38¹/₈")

Hartung, a German, was born in Leipzig in 1904, but has lived in France since 1934. He became a French citizen and was seriously wounded serving with the French army in 1944. In his work we find a blend of the exacting discipline that governs French art with what is best and most distinguished in Germanic poetry. His pictures, like a verse of Heine or a song of Schumann, vibrate always with a nostalgic emotion and are filled with a disturbing vision of the infinite spaces; they are such as open the gates of dream. Still, there is in him no trace of the literaty element and here he parts company with many Germanic painters, for whom the idea, the meaning, a philosophic message, signify more than achieving the painting as an end in itself. The effect of the French tradition on Hartung and his keen taste for Far Eastern art (the influence of Japanese calligraphy is evident in this picture) have impelled him to express his own message through the medium of painting. One result is the decisiveness of line as well as the dexterity and vigour we find in this canvas; others are the precision with which the tones are related one to another and the art with which, on the ochres of the background and amongst the blacks, he makes the single patch of clear blue shine out with so much emphasis. These influences are potent also in the beauty of the paint, exquisite as lacquer and showing a true perfection of workmanship.

Purchased from the artist by the State.

PIERRE SOULAGES (born 1919)   1957, signed and dated
PAINTING   Oil on canvas
                                              Height 194 cm. (76¹/₃″)
                                                Width 130 cm. (51″)

In abstract art as in figurative painting there is room for great variety, explained by the different trends within the movement and also by the individual characteristics of the artists who practise it. Even before 1914, there was lyric, intellectual, decorative, and Impressionist abstraction. It is possible to distinguish between one born of Cubism, one that is a continuation of Surrealism, one owing everything to Expressionism, one that carries further the poetic imagery of Klee, and so on.

The most valid of these forms are perhaps those that rely least on an *a priori* attitude or any partisan tenets. Moreover, those extensions of the geometric and ascetic Neo-Plasticism advocated by Vasarely, or the tendency to informalism that Mathieu fosters, have less hold than the form that might be described as the intention to be strictly plastic like the first, and, in the manner of the other, charged with human significance and with poetry. This particular form has attracted many remarkable painters, and Soulages is one of those who best expresses it. He was born in the Massif Central where ancient *menhirs* stand near Romanesque churches filled with great sculptured figures. These two art forms made a great impact on Soulages and influenced his painting decisively towards an austere and majestic style, a shade untamed, towards forcefulness and solemnity. He has a great liking for height and for shapes that rise up heavily. Drawing and colour are here merged; the brush that lays on the tones also gives them their contour. The colour-scale is sombre, with a basis of blacks, browns, sea-greens, night-sky blues and greys. The chiaroscuro varies, blends and enhances the tone, while by opening luminous gaps behind the interlaced 'signs' or devices, he places the shapes within a space that gives them life and poetry. The firm and spacious handling imparts a wholly authoritative quality to the paint, sometimes thick and sometimes transparent. The art of Soulages is complex and yet all of a piece; it distils from these two conflicting qualities a richness and force that put it in the front rank of modern abstract painting.

Shown at the Salon de Mai, 1957 (No. 192). Presented by the artist, 1957.

JEAN-MICHEL ATLAN (1913–1960)　　　　　Signed
Le Kahéna　　　　　　　　　　　　　　　　Oil on canvas
　　　　　　　　　　　　　　　　Height 146 cm. (57³/₈")
　　　　　　　　　　　　　　　　Width 89 cm. (35")

Like Hartung and Soulages, Atlan is a painter who is solely and entirely abstract. His pictures are not, like those of Bazaine and Manessier, the transposing of some natural spectacle on to a plane where it is no longer possible to recognize it. He does not 'take off' from the natural object but from the canvas and from his own private self, covering the surface with lines, colours and shapes that bear no relation to the perceptible world, and in this way expressing his own inner life. It is an inner life that is strangely sad, that seems as if darkened by the prospect of his own untimely death and haunted by visions that make him, as it were, the Odilon Redon of abstract art. Atlan, a Jew from Constantine, steeped in the Bible and the Talmud, as well as in Berber folklore (from which he takes the name of *Kahéna* for this painting), was still strongly affected by the influences of his childhood. These are very apparent in this painting: there are the pointed shapes, like those of the cactus of North Africa, the tawny colours recalling the burnt earth, and the light, heavy in its blinding glow. All these factors are made to serve Atlan in his search for the ultimate perfection, and this makes each of his canvases an attempt to gain a greater knowledge of himself and of the mysteries of life. As a result his painting has a tension that finds its parallel in Van Gogh, a tragic quality that has a tinge of hallucination and a kind of grandeur that is indeed uncommon.

　Purchased by the State from the artist, 1958.

NICOLAS DE STAËL (1914–1955)   1952, signed and dated
THE ROOFS   Oil on isorel
Height 200 cm. (78³/₄")
Width 150 cm. (59")

Staël died whilst still fairly young. He had one of the finest talents of the
new Ecole de Paris and is still one of the most potent influences on the
young painters of today. His earliest work was tentative but full of
promise (1937–1940); it was interrupted by the war and his enlistment in
the Foreign Legion. Then from 1942 to 1944 he drifted very gradually
towards abstract painting, and gave himself up to it with determination
soon after the end of the war. He went on to paint canvases unmatched in
power; the unerring handling, the authority of the execution, remind one
inevitably of Courbet. *Composition* (1949) in the Musée d'Art Moderne is
a characteristic work. However, he was beginning to grow out of sympathy
with the abstractionists. He looked towards an art that transcends both the
figurative and abstraction, and this he achieved, from 1951, in landscapes,
nudes and still-lifes. The two vast canvases of *Bottles in the Studio* are
the supreme product of this transitional period. *The Roofs*, earlier by some
months, will bear comparison with them. It was painted in January 1952
and is one of the most perfectly achieved of the important works painted
by Staël at this turning-point in his life. The subtle harmony of the predominant greys, blended with exquisite blues and given warmth by a dark
red, in no way detracts from the power given by the sweep of the execution. Staël, having taken to a coarse palette knife, laid on the tones with
a breadth and decision that are enough to place him in the forefront of
the painters of our time. Shortly afterwards he was to give up the muted
chromatism in which he had taken such pleasure since 1945. The many-
coloured spectacle of a football match at the Parc des Princes, the discovery of the landscape of the South of France and then of Sicily, were
to induce him to heighten the tones and, with a daring only justified by
the result, to bring together great streams of pure colour as vivid as they
were deep. Thereafter his art developed on more figurative lines, with a
swifter manner of painting, using quieter tones and a thinner pigment. This
development was cut short by his death, and it would be rather unfair to
let it be the measure of the painter of *The Roofs*, the *Souvenir de Sydney
Bechet,* and many other masterly works, achieved to perfection.

The painting was presented by the artist in 1952.

On the preceding pages are illustrated in colour
120 of the masterpieces of the School of Paris.
The monochrome reproductions that follow,
presented in chronological order, cover many of the other important
paintings in the Musée d'Art Moderne.

Charles Angrand
Man and woman in the street. 1887

Maximilien Luce The Seine at Herblay. 1890

Edouard Vuillard Woman darning. 1891

Henri Matisse Breton weaver. 1896

Maurice Denis The Mellerio family. 1897

Henri Matisse Provençal landscape, the pink wall. 1898

253

Pierre Bonnard Women and children. 1899

Félix Vallotton The Balloon. 1899

Pierre Bonnard
Man and woman. 1900

Henri-Edmond Cross Cypresses, Cagnes. 1900

Edouard Vuillard The breakfast table. c. 1900

Edouard Vuillard
Landscape at Etang-la-Ville. c. 1900

254

Paul Signac Le Palais des Papes, Avignon. 1900

Pablo Picasso
Portrait of M. Gustave Coquiot. c. 1901

Achille Laugé Landscape, La Gardie. 1902

Raoul Dufy The beach at Sainte-Adresse. 1904

Jean Puy Landscape, Saint-Alban-les-Eaux. c. 1904

255

Edouard Vuillard Vase of flowers. 1904

Maurice de Vlaminck Street scene, Marly-le-Roi. 1904

Auguste Chabaud
The Moulin de la Galette. 1905

Maurice de Vlaminck
The kitchen. 1905

Maurice de Vlaminck Hillside at Rueil. 1906

Pierre Bonnard In the boat. 1907

Maurice Denis
On the balcony, Venice. 1907

Maurice Marinot
Young woman and child. c. 1907

Maurice Utrillo Roofs. c. 1907

Georges Braque Landscape, Estaque. 1908

Edouard Vuillard
Portrait of Mme Suzanne Desprès. 1908

Henry Le Fauconnier Portrait of the poet
Pierre-Jean Jouve. 1909

257

Henry Matisse Algerian woman. 1909

Francis Picabia Rubber. 1909

Robert Delaunay The Town. 1910

Roger de La Fresnaye Nudes in a Landscape. 1910

Maurice Utrillo Le Lapin Agile. 1910

Maurice Utrillo L'impasse Cottin. c. 1910

Georges Rouault
The steps in the Parc de Versailles. 1910

Maurice de Vlaminck Poplars. 1910

Maurice de Vlaminck Le Pont de Chatou. 1910

Louis Valtat Gladioli and aconites. 1910

Georges Braque Side table. 1911

Robert Delaunay The towers of Laon. 1911

Roger de La Fresnaye Landscape, La Ferté-sous-Jouarre. 1911

Roger de La Fresnaye
Still-life with egg-cup. 1911

Kees van Dongen La grille de l'Elysée. c. 1912

Kees van Dongen Les Fellahs. c. 1912

Maurice Denis Paradise. 1912

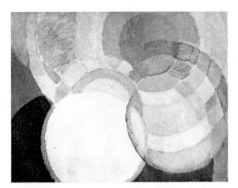

Frank Kupka Discs. c. 1912

Albert Marquet Le Pont Saint-Michel. 1912

Albert Marquet Woman on a Sofa. 1912

Alfred Reth Le restaurant Hubin. 1912

Roger de La Fresnaye The 14th July. 1914

Fernand Léger Woman in red and green. 1914

Albert Marquet Rotterdam. 1914

Pablo Picasso The Violin. 1914

Suzanne Valadon Fishermen casting nets. 1914

Albert Gleizes. Portrait of Florent Schmitt. 1915

Juan Gris Breakfast. 1915

Maurice Utrillo La rue du Mont-Cenis. 1915

Robert Delaunay Woman pouring milk, Portugese still-life. 1915—16

Amedeo Modigliani Caryatid. c. 1914—16

Henri Matisse La route de Clamart. 1917

André Lhote Rugby. 1917

André Lhote Portrait face et profil. 1917

Juan Gris Pierrot. 1919

263

Marie Laurencin Women with dove. 1919

Pierre Laprade Corn. 1919

Georges Braque Black side table. 1919

Jean Metzinger Woman knitting. 1919

Charles Dufresne Tropical forest. 1919

Raoul Dufy Three bathers. 1919

Pierre Bonnard
Portrait of the brothers Bernheim de Villers. 1920

Henri Hayden Three musicians. 1920

Suzanne Valadon Vase of flowers. 1920

Pablo Picasso Woman in grey, reading. 1920

Yves Alix The master of the harvest. 1921

Maria Blanchard Maternité. 1921

Pierre Bonnard Beach at low tide. c. 1922

Pierre Bonnard
La toilette. c. 1922

Henri Matisse Odalisque in red pantaloons. 1922

Suzanne Valadon
La femme à la commode. 1922

Léonard Foujita
Interior of my room, Paris. 1922

Camille Bombois Le Pont de Chablis. c. 1923

Louis Vivin
Rheims Cathedral. c. 1923

Othon Friesz Portrait of Mme Othon Friesz. 1923

Albert Gleizes Composition. 1920—23

Roger de La Fresnaye
Portrait of Guynemer. 1921—23

Suzanne Valadon The blue room. 1923

267

Maurice-Albert Loutreuil
Still-life with Chianti bottle. 1923

Félix Vallotton House and reeds. c. 1921—24

Pierre Bonnard
Panorama, Le Cannet. 1924

Edouard Vuillard
Portrait of Henri-Xavier Fontaine. c. 1924

Pierre Bonnard The red bodice. 1925

Kees van Dongen
Portrait of Mme Jasmy Alvin. 1925

Juan Gris Siphon and basket. 1925

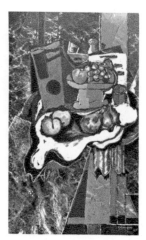

Georges Braque
Still-life with marble table. 1925

Louis Marcoussis Still-life with goldfish. 1925

Pablo Picasso Still-life with antique head. 1925

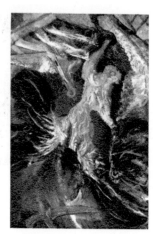

Chaïm Soutine Poultry. 1925—26

Amédée de La Patellière
The rest in the cellar. 1926

André Derain The forest of Fontainbleau. 1927

André Dunoyer de Segonzac Saint-Tropez. 1927

Henri Matisse Decorative figure
on an ornamental ground. c. 1927

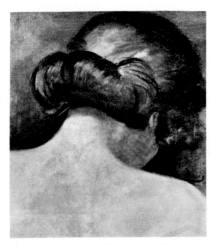

André Derain The blonde. 1928

Amédée de La Patellière The cowherd. 1928

Moïse Kisling
Woman in a Polish shawl. c. 1928

Luc-Albert Moreau
The bedroom of neighbours. 1928

Max Ernst Composition. 1929

Jules Pascin Two women asleep. 1929

Pierre Bonnard Landscape with tug. c. 1930

Pierre Bonnard Mountain landscape,
Provençal scene, Le Cannet. 1929—30

Maurice Brianchon
Women at their toilet. 1930

Othon Friesz Dieppe harbour. 1930

Marc Chagall The Acrobat. 1930

André Lhote The 14th July at Avignon. 1930

Joan Miró Landscape. 1930

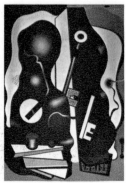

Fernand Léger
Still-life with keys. 1930

Edouard Vuillard Portrait of Mme Bénard. c. 1930

Jacques Villon Amro. 1931

Pierre Bonnard
Corner of the dining room, Le Cannet. c. 1932

André Dunoyer de Segonzac
La Route de Meaux à Couilly. 1932

Fernand Léger Composition with three figures. 1932

Pierre Roy Indian summer. 1932

André Marchand The Unknown. 1935

Roland Oudot The tarmac road. c. 1935

Pablo Picasso The Muse. 1935

Jacques Villon The Adventure. 1935

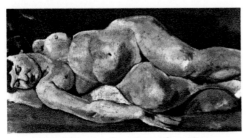

François Desnoyer Recumbent nude. c. 1936

André Dunoyer de Segonzac
Still-life with bread and wine. c. 1936

274

Wassily Kandinsky Composition. 1936

Louis Marcoussis Table in front of a balcony. 1936

Albert Marquet Venice, the Lagoon. 1936

André Masson Bloodshed. 1936

Roger Bissière
Standing figure. 1937

Raoul Dufy La Fée électricité. 1937

Charles Dufresne The sacrifice of Iphigenea. c. 1936—37

Marcel Gromaire The Forest. 1937

Yves Tanguy The slowness of days. 1937

Jaques Villon Woman in red. 1937

Pablo Picasso Portrait of a woman. 1938

Henri Matisse Woman reading, black background. 1939

Georges Braque La Carafe. 1941

Henri Matisse
Two friends. 1941

Raymond Legueult Woman with a rose. c. 1941   *Pablo Picasso* Portrait of Mme Paul Eluard. 1941

Henri Jannot Still-life. 1942   *Georges Braque* Black fish. 1942

Georges Braque The green cloth. 1943

Marc Chagall War. 1943

Pablo Picasso The rocking-chair. 1943

Georges Braque Le Salon. 1944

Marc Chagall To my wife. 1933—44

Pablo Picasso Woman in blue. 1944

Léon Gischa Canvases. 1944

Auguste Herbin Air, fire. 1944

Charles Walch The Canal. 1944

Christian Caillard
White house, Saint-Guénolé. 1945

Lucien Coutaud The green skirt. 1945

Félix Labisse The destiny of the prince. 1945

279

Marc Chagall The spirit of the town. 1945

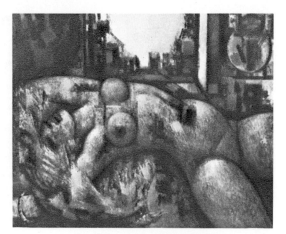

Marcel Gromaire Russian woman. 1945

Francis Gruber Woman on a sofa. 1945

Bernard Buffet Pietà. 1946

Jacques Despierre Huntsmen. 1946

Jean Eve
The quarry at Ville-d'Avray, from the lake. 1946

Georges Rouault
The flight into Egypt. c. 1946

Georges Rouault
Landscape with tall trees. c. 1946

Georges Rouault
Idle dream. c. 1946

Georges Rouault
De Profundis. c. 1946

Fernand Léger Adieu, New York. 1946

Roger Bissière Pastoral. 1946

281

Yves Brayer The plain of Les Baux, Provence. 1947

Alfred Manessier Blue harbour. 1948

Georges Rouault
The Passion. 1949

André Lanskoy Multitudes. 1949

Pierre Tal-Coat
Composition; Fish. c. 1949

Fernand Léger Leisure (Homage to Louis David). 1948—49

282

Gérard Schneider Abstract. 1950

Nicolas de Staël Le Lavandou. 1952

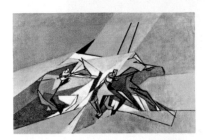

André Beaudin The first race. 1952

Georges Mathieu Les Capétiens partout. 1954

Daniel Ravel
Dives harbour at night. 1954

Zao-Wou-Ki Fire. 1954

Roger Chastel The 14th July at Toulon. 1955

Gustave Singier
Egyptian Nocturne. 1955

Léon Zack Composition. 1955

Georges Rohner Potato diggers. 1956

Arpad Szenes Landscape. 1958

Jean Cortot La Correspondance. 1959

Vieira da Silva Summer. 1960

284

PAINTERS OF THE SCHOOL OF PARIS

ALIX, YVES, born at Fontainebleau 19th August 1890. Student at the Ecole des Beaux-Arts, then at the Académie Ranson. After the 1914 War drawn to Expressionism, from which he broke away by degrees after the 1939 War, to achieve a form of painting at once calmer and with more colour and construction.

ANGRAND, CHARLES, born at Criquetot-sur-Ouville (Seine Maritime) 29th April, 1854, died at Rouen 1st April 1926. He was one of the founders of the Salon des Indépendants in 1884 and an exponent of Neo-Impressionism, which he later abandoned, after giving the best of his talents to it.

ATLAN, JEAN-MICHEL, born at Constantine 23rd January 1913, died in Paris 12th February 1960. Coming late to painting, after brilliant studies in philosophy and an interesting start in writing, he almost immediately devoted himself to abstract art, to which he gives a visionary and poetic form. Galerie Maeght, 1947, Galerie Bing, 1956, Musée d'Antibes, 1957. Musée d'Art Moderne retrospective exhibition, 1962.

BAUCHANT, ANDRÉ, born 1873 at Châteaurenault (Indre et Loire), died at Montoire August 1958. After being a gardener he gave himself up to painting in 1918, worked for the Russian Ballet, attracted the interest of the Galerie Jeanne Bucher to his art. Large-scale exhibition at the Galerie Charpentier in 1948.

BAZAINE, JEAN, born in Paris 21st December 1904. Gained distinction in his secondary and higher education. Pupil of Landowski at the Ecole des Beaux-Arts. Finding his definite vocation in painting, he was awarded the Prix Blumenthal in 1938 and in 1941 became one of the organisers of the exhibition of the Jeunes Peintres de Tradition Française. His work, hung in the Galerie Carré (1943), then in the Galerie Maeght (1949), brought him an international reputation. Worked in stained glass and mosaics (church at Audincourt, UNESCO House in Paris) and wrote the first-rate *Notes sur la peinture d'aujourd'-hui* (2nd edition 1953).

BEAUDIN, ANDRÉ, born 3rd February 1895 at Mennecy (Seine et Oise). Ecole des Arts Décoratifs (1911–1913). An admirer of Cubism and during the inter-war years advocated the claims of pure painting. Kahnweiler became interested in this artist, who exhibited mainly at his gallery and then at the Galerie Louise Leiris.

BERNARD, EMILE, born at Lille 28th April 1868, died in Paris 16th April, 1941. One of the strangest stories in the history of painting. A friend of Toulouse-Lautrec, of Seurat, Signac, Van Gogh, Gauguin and later, of Cézanne. As a very young man he laid the foundations of Cloisonnism and Synthesism, to which he may quite likely have introduced Gauguin. Then, after a period of intense creativeness in *avant-garde* painting, from about 1887 to 1895, he broke away from modern art, and turned to the traditions of the Renaissance Venetians, on which he modelled himself until his death, challenging contemporary painting in many articles and reviews, especially in *La Rénovation Esthétique*.

BISSIÈRE, ROGER (also known as a designer of wall hangings and stained glass), born 22nd September 1888 at Villeréal (Lot et Garonne). He came to Paris in 1910, was a member of the team of *Esprit Nouveau,* for which he wrote, and taught at the Académie Ranson from 1925 to 1938. He withdrew to Boissierette (Lot) from 1939 to 1945 and was late in making his reputation. Grand Prix National des Arts in 1952. The Musée d'Art Moderne retrospective exhibition in 1959 provided evidence of his distinction and talent.

BLANCHARD, MARIA, born 1881 at Santander, Spain (father Spanish, mother half French, half Polish). Died in Paris in 1932. Hunchbacked from birth. Studied in Madrid, then in Paris from 1908 to 1913. Returned to France in 1916. Influenced by Cubism. She excelled in capturing the poignant mystery of scenes of family life and of children.

BOMBOIS, CAMILLE, born at Vénarey-les-Laumes (Côte d'Or) 3rd February, 1883. Farm hand, 'strong man' at a fair and navvy; he took up painting in 1922. Singled out by the collector Wilhelm Uhde, he is one of the principal 'twentieth-century primitives'.

BONNARD, PIERRE, born at Fontenay-aux-Roses (Seine) 30th October, 1867, died at Le Cannet (Alpes Maritimes) 23rd January, 1947. Académie Julian, and Nabi group, where he was nicknamed the 'Japanese Nabi'. Nabi style from about 1891 to 1899. Then came under the influence of Impressionism and turned towards colour, which he was to use better than any of his contemporaries.

BOUSSINGAULT, JEAN-LOUIS, born in Paris 8th March, 1883, died in Paris 17th May, 1943. Ecole des Arts Décoratifs. Became a friend of Dunoyer de Segonzac (1902). Académie Julian. Académie La Palette, where he came to know L. A. Moreau. With these two friends, one of the main champions of the Neo-Realism that came to the fore immediately after the 1914 War.

BRAQUE, GEORGES, born at Argenteuil (Seine) 13th May 1882. Childhood at Le Havre where he was friendly with Dufy and Friesz. Ecole des Beaux-Arts at Le Havre. Académie Humbert in Paris. Fauve Group (1906). The influence of Cézanne gave his painting more construction. The example of the *Demoiselles d'Avignon* by Picasso, with whom he had a lively friendship from 1908 to 1914, led to their working out together the basis of Cubism. Called up in 1914, wounded and invalided out in 1917. Returning to painting he remained true to an advanced form of Cubism, which he carried to its final conclusions. Prix International of painting at the Venice Biennale in 1948.

BRAYER, YVES, born at Versailles 18th November 1907. Ecole des Beaux-Arts. Scholarship for visit to Spain (1927), where he was influenced by Solana. Grand Prix de Rome in 1930. Member of the Académie des Beaux-Arts.

BRIANCHON, MAURICE, born at Fresnay-sur-Sarthe 3rd January 1899. Ecole des Beaux-Arts of Bordeaux, Ecole des Arts Décoratifs in Paris, where he joined forces with Oudot and Legueult. Prix Blumenthal, 1924, Prix Carnegie, 1935. Teacher at the Ecole des Arts Décoratifs in 1937, then at the Ecole des Beaux-Arts. One of the chief '*peintres de la réalité poétique*'.

BUFFET, BERNARD, born 10th July 1928 in Paris. Ecole des Beaux-Arts (1944). Prix de la Critique jointly with Lorjou (1948). Numerous exhibitions at the Galerie Drouant-David, then at the Galerie David et Garnier.

286

CAILLARD, CHRISTIAN, born at Clichy (Seine) 26th July 1899. Académie Biloul, where he was a friend of Dabit (1921). Met Loutreuil in 1923, with whom he worked at the Pré St Gervais. Prix Blumenthal, 1934. Travelled in Indo-China, Martinique, Spain, Morocco, Mexico, etc. He was a leading exponent of *'réalité poétique'*.

CAMOIN, CHARLES, born at Marseilles 23rd September 1879. A pupil of Moreau at the Ecole des Beaux-Arts, where he was a friend of Marquet. Fauve Group. In touch with Cézanne during his military service at Aix-en-Provence. Travelled in Morocco with Matisse and Marquet (1912). During the 1914 War a friend of Renoir, who strongly influenced him.

CHABAUD, AUGUSTE, born at Nîmes 3rd October 1882, and died at Graveson (Bouches-du-Rhône) 23rd May 1955. Exponent of Fauvism. Later settled in Provence; he never tired of painting its landscape and peasants.

CHAGALL, MARC, born 7th July 1887 at Vitebsk in Russia of a Jewish family. Studied at the Petrograd Academy. Came to Paris in 1911 and lodged at La Ruche, became friends with Modigliani, Delaunay, Apollinaire, Max Jacob, Cendrars. Large-scale exhibition, *Sturm* gallery, Berlin, in 1914. Returned to Russia, married there 1915, appointed Commissar for Fine Arts, 1917. From 1922 until the Nazi Occupation lived in Paris. Then in the United States. In Paris again in 1947, and acquired French citizenship. Large scale exhibitions, Musée d'Art Moderne (1947), Musée des Arts Décoratifs (1959 and 1961). Prix International of the Venice Biennale in 1948.

CHASTEL, ROGER, born in Paris 25th March 1897. Académie Julian. Influenced first by Cubism, then by Neo-Realism. Since the 1939 War he has been developing a greater boldness in his art, and was awarded the Prix International of painting at the First Biennale of Sao Paulo (1951).

CORTOT, JEAN, born in Alexandria 14th February 1925. Adopted son of the famous pianist. Pupil of Friesz, in whose studio he joined forces with painters of the Echelle group, such as Calmettes, Patrix, Dalmbert and especially Busse. Prix de la Jeune Peinture in 1948.

COUTAUD, LUCIEN, born at Meynes (Gard) 13th December 1904. Ecole des Beaux-Arts of Nîmes. Private art schools in Paris, where he was influenced by Surrealism. Did a great deal of work for the theatre, for Dullin (*Les Oiseaux,* 1928), Copeau (*Comme il vous plaira,* 1939), Barrault (*Le soulier de satin,* 1943).

CROSS, HENRI-EDMOND, *real name* DELACROIX, born at Douai 20th March 1856 and died at Saint Clair, near Le Lavandou (Var), 16th May 1910. Ecole des Beaux-Arts of Lille. In Paris pupil of Bonvin. Founder in 1884 of the Salon des Indépendants. The chief exponent of Neo-Impressionism, together with Seurat and Signac. Like them, he was at his best in his masterly water-colours.

DALI, SALVADOR, born 11th March 1904 at Figueras (Catalonia), was attached to the School of Paris during 1928–1940, then turned to Surrealism. First visited the United States in 1934, long stay there during the Second World War. Returning to Spain, he cut a figure as official painter and produced religious works in an extremely traditional style.

DELAUNAY, ROBERT, born in Paris 12th April 1885, died at Montpellier 25th October 1941. Influenced first by Neo-Impressionism, then by Cézanne. Short period of Cubism (*Cities* series). Founder, with his wife Sonia Terk, of the movement which Apollinaire in 1913 named Orphic Cubism and which had a widespread repercussion in Germany on the painters of the *Blaue Reiter*, Franz Marc, August Macke and Paul Klee. One of the first exponents of abstract art (*Circular Forms* series, 1912–1914). In Spain and Portugal during the 1914 War. After his return to France his work was sometimes figurative and sometimes abstract (*Circular Rhythms* series), but always had the grandeur of concept seen in his decorations for the Pavilions of Railways and Aeronautics at the International Exhibition of 1937.

DELAUNAY, SONIA TERK, born in the Ukraine in 1885. Studied in Petrograd, then in Germany. Came to Paris in 1904. In 1910 married Robert Delaunay, with whom she had worked out Orphic Cubism. Took up book-binding and textile design. One of the first exponents of abstract art. (*La Prose du Trans-Sibérien*, 1913). After a stay in Spain and Portugal returned to Paris, where she remained more resolutely attached than her husband to abstract formulas.

DENIS, MAURICE, born at Granville 25th November 1870, died in Paris 1943. Académie Julian, where he became a friend of Sérusier (1888). Nabi Group. Two visits to Italy drew his interest to the Italian Primitives, then to Raphael, and so brought him towards a 'Neo-Traditionalism' to which can be traced most of the great murals, nearly all religious, that he began to do in 1910. Founder, with Desvallières, of the Ateliers d'Art Sacré in 1919. Elected to the Académie des Beaux-Arts in 1932.

DERAIN, ANDRÉ, born at Chatou (Seine et Oise) 10th June 1880, died at Garches 2nd September 1954. At the Académie Carrière, where he made friends with Matisse while coming to know Vlaminck at Chatou. Fauve Group. The influence of Cézanne and of Negro sculpture brought him to the fringes of Cubism about 1908–1910; that of the Douanier Rousseau and of Gothic art drew him towards the archaic. After the 1914 War he drifted into a traditional style, — inspired at different times by Corot, the Carracci, and Pompeian art – from which he escapes in his sculpture and his illustrations (the *Satyricon, Pantagruel*).

DESNOS, FERNAND, born at Pontlevoy (Loir et Cher) 1901, died in Paris 1958. Employed by the newspaper *L'Intransigeant*, then a concierge in Paris. He is one of the most recently discovered 'twentieth-century primitives'.

DESNOYER, FRANÇOIS, born at Montauban 30 September 1894. Ecole des Arts Décoratifs (1912–1913). After the 1914 War was associated with Walch: the two were like brothers. Prix Blumenthal in 1924. Teacher at the Ecole des Arts Décoratifs. Has been living at Sète for some years.

DESPIERRE, JACQUES, born at Saint Etienne 7th March 1912. Son of the painter Ceria. Académie Colarossi, then Académie Scandinave, where he was a pupil of Dufresne. Prix Paul Guillaume. Teacher at the Ecole des Arts Décoratifs.

DONGEN, KEES VAN, born at Delfshaven (Holland) 26th January 1877. Came to Paris at twenty and acquired French citizenship. Was associated with the Fauves before the 1914 War. Became eventually the recognized and savagely unsparing portraitist of Paris Society during the feverish post-war years.

DUCHAMP, MARCEL, born at Blainville (Seine Maritime) 28th July 1887. Younger brother of Jacques Villon and Raymond Duchamp-Villon, whom he influenced to join the Cubists about 1910. He himself withdrew from Cubism in 1912 *(Nude descending a staircase)* and went on to withdraw from art altogether, to become the chief advocate of 'anti-art', thus anticipating the Dadaists. In 1914 he settled in the United States and took American citizenship. After 1920 he gave up painting almost entirely to devote himself to chess.

DUFRESNE, CHARLES, born 23rd November 1876 at Millemont (Seine et Oise), died 8th August 1938 at La Seyne (Var). Ecole des Beaux-Arts. Prix de la Villa Abd-el-Tif in 1910. Spent much time in Algeria, where he found himself as a painter. During the 1914 War was in the Camouflage section with Dunoyer de Segonzac, L. A. Moreau, Boussingault and Charles Vildrac. Teacher at the Académie Scandinave. From an art carefully structural, sombre and static, he passed to one full of colour, luminous, baroque, and essentially decorative (Palais de Chaillot, Ecole de Pharmacie).

DUFY, RAOUL, born at Le Havre 3rd June 1877, died at Forcalquier (Basses Alpes) 23rd March 1953. Evening classes, Ecole des Beaux-Arts of Le Havre. Scholarship from Le Havre to Paris, Ecole des Beaux-Arts (in the class of Bonnat) together with his friend Friesz. Matisse's work converted him to Fauvism. Came under the influence of Cézannism in 1909 after a visit to Munich with Friesz, and his style became structural and sombre. Earned his living by wood-engraving, designs for fabrics commissioned by Poiret and later Bianchini, and ceramics. About 1925 his art became freer and more elegant. Returned to the grand scale with his decorative panels for the Pavilion of Electricity at the International Exhibition of 1937, and also in his last style, called 'tonal' – defying the crippling rheumatism that compelled him to seek a cure at Perpignan, then in Boston and finally at Forcalquier.

DUNOYER DE SEGONZAC, ANDRÉ, born 16th July 1884 at Boussy Saint Antoine (Seine et Oise). Académie La Palette. Friend of Boussingault and L. A. Moreau, then, in the Camouflage section during the war, of Dufresne. The leading advocate of Neo-Realism, he painted in oils and in water-colour (in which he excelled) and did drawings and engravings, especially of the landscapes of Saint Tropez, powerful nudes and vigorous still-lifes.

ERNST, MAX, born at Brühl, Germany, 1891. Promoted the Dada movement in Cologne in 1919. Came to Paris in 1920 and took up Surrealism. In the United States during the Second World War. Returned to France 1953, French citizenship 1958. Prix International of painting at the Venice Biennale of 1954. Prix National des Arts in 1959. Important retrospective exhibition, Musée d'Art Moderne, 1959.

ESTÈVE, MAURICE, born at Culan (Cher) 2nd May 1904. Came to Paris about 1919, Académie Colarossi. Typographer, then director of a design section at a Barcelona textile factory (1923). On returning to France, exhibited at the Salons d'Automne, des Tuileries and des Surindépendants. An associate of Pignon and with him in 1941 took part in the exhibition of the Jeunes Peintres de Tradition Française. Exhibited at the Galerie Carré, then the Galerie Galanis.

EVE, JEAN, born at Somain (Nord) 1900. Apprentice in machine shop; quantity surveyor and draughtsman; foundry-worker; in a motor-car factory; on the railways, and then in an *octroi* toll-house. He never ceased to paint, however.

First exhibition 1930. In 1937 took part in the Exhibition of the Maîtres populaires de la Réalité, where his talent was recognized.

FOUJITA, LÉONARD, born at Edogawa, Japan, 27th November 1886. Imperial School of Fine Arts of Tokyo. Came to Paris in 1913. Member of the Academy of Fine Arts of Tokyo (1924). Returned to Japan at outbreak of Second World War. To France again in 1950. Became a Christian and changed his first name from Tsuguharu to Léonard, in honour of Leonardo da Vinci.

FRIESZ, EMILE-OTHON, born at Le Havre 6th February 1879, died in Paris 10th January 1949. Evening classes, Ecole des Beaux-Arts at Le Havre, where he became friendly with Dufy. Scholarship to the Ecole des Beaux-Arts in Paris (class of Bonnat). Associated with Dufy and Braque and, like them, took up Fauvism, but gave it up about 1909, influenced by Cézanne. After the 1914 War gradually turned towards a traditionalist realism inspired by the baroque.

GISCHIA, LÉON, born at Dax (Landes) 8th June 1904. Came to Paris, pupil of Léger. Stayed in the United States in 1927. Worked with Léger and Le Corbusier on decoration of the Pavilion of Modern Times at the International Exhibition of 1937. In the exhibition of the Jeunes Peintres de Tradition Française, 1941. Hung at the Galerie de France, then at the Galerie Galanis. He did much work for the theatre, with some fine scene-painting for the productions of Jean Vilar.

GLEIZES, ALBERT, born in Paris 8th December 1881, died at Avignon 23rd June 1953. Took up Cubism about 1909 and his studio at Courbevoie became one of its chief centres. In 1912, with Metzinger, published the famous *Du Cubisme*. After the 1914 War he was drawn to abstract painting. Was prime mover in colony of artists at Moly-Sabata near Vienne (Isère) and later of a group of painters who came to settle near him at Saint Rémy (Provence), where he lived from 1939 until his death.

GOERG, EDOUARD, born in Sydney 9th June 1893. French and Irish parents. Came to France when he was seven years old. Académie Ranson. Friendly about 1924 with Gromaire and Pascin, who shared his Expressionism. Prix Hallmark in 1949. Teacher of engraving at the Ecole des Beaux-Arts.

GRIS, JOSÉ GONZALES, known as JUAN, born in Madrid 23rd March 1887, died at Boulogne-sur-Seine 11th May 1927. School of Arts and Crafts in Madrid. Came to Paris in 1906. Closely associated with Picasso who converted him to analytical Cubism. Later, with Picasso he created synthetic Cubism (1913–1914). Hung at the Galerie Kahnweiler; 1923 full-scale exhibition of his works there.

GROMAIRE, MARCEL, born at Noyelles-sur-Sambre (Nord) 24th July 1892. Pupil of Le Fauconnier at the Académie La Palette, who led him towards Expressionism. His interest in decorative art was fulfilled in his decoration of the Sèvres Pavilion at the International Exhibition of 1937 and his tapestry designs for the Aubusson workshops, which, with Lurçat, he saved from decline just before the Second World War. Prix National des Arts.

GRUBER, FRANCIS, born at Nancy 15th March 1912, died in Paris 1st December 1948. Son and brother of stained glass artists. In Paris, at the Académie Scandinave, a pupil of Friesz and Dufresne. Very early success (decoration of the Lycée Lakanal, 1936). Prix National des Arts in 1947. Musée d'Art Moderne retrospective exhibition in 1949, after his premature death. He has had a great posthumous influence on the *'misérabiliste'* painters, Bernard Buffet in particular.

HARTUNG, HANS, born at Leipzig 21st September 1904. Acquired French nationality in 1945, after having been wounded in the French army before Belfort, when he lost a leg. Brilliant record in his secondary and advanced studies. Academies of Fine Arts of Leipzig and Dresden. Abstract painter since 1922. Travelled throughout Europe. When the Nazis came to power, he settled in Paris, where he has remained except for the war years, partly spent in Algeria. Hung at the Galerie Lydia Conti in 1947, then at the Galerie Carré and later at the Galerie de France. Shared with Fautrier the Prix International of painting at the Venice Biennale of 1960.

HAYDEN, HENRI, born in Warsaw 24th December 1888. School of Fine Arts of Warsaw. Came to Paris in 1907. Académie La Palette. Influenced by Cézanne and then by Cubism. Later returned to an art of greater realism. Became a French citizen.

HERBIN, AUGUSTE, born at Guévy (Nord) 29th April 1882, died in Paris 31st January 1960. Ecole des Beaux-Arts of Lille. Came to Paris in 1903. Took up Cubism about 1910. After the 1914 War went on to geometric abstract painting, from which nothing could deflect him. (He gave an account of it in *L'Art non-figuratif, non-objectif,* 1949.)

JANNOT, HENRI, born in Paris 27th January 1905. Ecole des Beaux-Arts (Lucien Simon class). An associate of Humblot, Rohner and Lasne, with whom he formed the *Forces Nouvelles* group. Their work was first brought before the public by Henri Héraut in 1935. It showed a distinct reaction against the delicate art of Brianchon and Legueult, harking back to Uccello, Piero della Francesca, Zurbarán and Georges de la Tour.

KANDINSKY, WASSILI, born in Moscow 5th December 1866. Died at Neuilly-sur-Seine 13th December 1944. Advanced studies in polititical economy at the University of Moscow (1884). Decided to give himself up to painting and set out for Munich (1896). Stayed in Sèvres (1906), in Berlin and Dresden (1907). Founded the New Association of Munich Artists (1909). Started the *Blaue Reiter* movement (first exhibition in Munich, December 1911). Published his book *Über das Geistige in der Kunst* (1911) and his poem *Klänge* (1913). Returned to Russia in 1914 where he became teacher at the Academy of Fine Arts of Moscow (1918) and also head of the Academy of Arts and Sciences (1921). Left for Berlin in December 1921. Instructor at the *Bauhaus* in Weimar (1922–1925), then at Dessau (1925–1931). Settled at Neuilly-sur-Seine (December 1933). Became a French citizen in 1939.

KISLING, MOÏSE, born at Cracow 22nd January 1891, died at Sanary (Var) 29th April 1953. Jewish. Academy of Cracow, pupil of Pankiewicz. Came to Paris in 1910. Influenced by Cézanne and Derain. After serving in the Foreign Legion during the 1914 War, thus taking French citizenship, he painted in a very personal version of Expressionism, brilliant in colour with sharply defined drawing.

KUPKA, FRANK, born at Opocno (Bohemia) 23rd September 1871 and died at Puteaux 21st June, 1957. Studied in Prague, then Vienna. Came to Paris in 1894.

One of the originators of abstract painting (*Amorpha, Fugue in two colours* 1912). Remained faithful to abstraction. The high quality of his work only became appreciated with the posthumous exhibition at the Musée d'Art Moderne in 1958.

LABISSE, FÉLIX, born at Douai 9th March 1905. Influenced by Surrealism. Undertook some remarkable designing for the theatre, especially for Jean-Louis Barrault.

LA FRESNAYE, ROGER DE, born at Le Mans 11th July, 1885 and died at Grasse November 27th 1925. Académie Julian, then Académie Ranson. Influenced by Gauguin, later by Cézanne. Took up Cubism about 1911 and attended the gatherings in the Villon brothers' studio at Puteaux. Took part in the movement of the *Section d'Or.* Joined up as a volunteer in 1914, was gassed in 1917, evacuated to Tours. Contracted tuberculosis and went from one sanatorium to another. Was obliged to give up painting in oils for work in gouache and drawings.

LANSKOY, ANDRÉ, born in Moscow 31st March 1902. Came to Paris in 1921. Gradually turned to abstraction from 1937. Shown at the Galerie Carré. Works also in tapestry.

LA PATELLIÈRE, AMÉDÉE DE, born at Bois-Benoît (Loire Maritime) 5th July 1890 and died in Paris 9th January, 1932. Did well in his secondary and advanced education. Came to Paris in 1912. Académie Julian. Received wounds in the 1914 War which led to his early death. Wholly independent in his art, which is both realist and visionary, with a strange poetry; at first he prefered muted colours, but after staying at Saint Paul de Vence, he used a much brighter range. Full-scale retrospective exhibition at Musée d'Art Moderne in 1945.

LAPICQUE, CHARLES, born at Théizé (Rhône) 6th October 1898 of a scholarly family. Educated at the Ecole Centrale. Member of the Faculty of Sciences in the University of Paris. Paintings first shown in 1925 at the Galerie Jeanne Bucher. In 1941, took part in the exhibition of the Jeunes Peintres de Tradition Française with Bazaine, and with Estève, whose experiments he mapped out and with whom he exhibited at the Galerie Carré. Later at the Galerie Galanis. Long spells in Italy, which rivals Brittany in his affections and in his painting.

LAPRADE, PIERRE, born at Narbonne 25th Juli 1875, died at Fontenay-aux-Roses 23rd December 1931. Developed independently in Paris. Ambroise Vollard took a great interest in him. He cannot be assigned to any school; his art is realist and has a delicate lyricism inspired by Italy, and by Watteau who makes him a kind of forerunner of the painters of the so-called '*réalité poétique*'.

LAUGÉ, ACHILLE, born at Argens (Aude) 29th April 1861, died at Cailhau (Aude) 12th June 1944. Ecole des Beaux-Arts in Paris, where he was friendly with Bourdelle and Maillol (1881). He became converted to Neo-Impressionism (1888) and was its ardent exponent in Languedoc, where he returned in 1889. Exhibited in Paris in 1907, 1919, 1923, 1927, 1929, 1930. Designs for Gobelin tapestries (1913–1920).

LAURENCIN, MARIE, born in Paris 31st October 1888, died in Paris 8th June 1956. Ecole de Sèvres and studied painting at the Académie Humbert. A great friend of Apollinaire, she was introduced by him into Cubist circles and came under the influence of Negro art. After the 1914 War, her great success in the social world did much to encourage her filmy and elegant painting. She also did some first-rate *décors* for the theatre.

LE CORBUSIER, real name Edouard Jeanneret, born at La Chaux de Fonds (Switzerland) 6th October 1887. Studied in Switzerland, Austria, and in France in the studio of Perret. In 1920, with Ozenfant, he founded the Purist movement, with its review, *L'Esprit Nouveau*. His great fame as an architect has overshadowed, unjustly, his work as a painter, sculptor and designer of tapestry. The Musée d'Art Moderne held an exhibition of his work in 1953.

LE FAUCONNIER, HENRI, born at Hesdin (Pas de Calais) 1881, died in Paris January 1946. Académie Julian. Exponent of Cubism from 1910. Teacher at the Académie La Palette, where he encouraged a kind of Expressionism. His wide international reputation took him to the Netherlands, where he remained for the duration of the 1914 War, exercising a decisive influence on Dutch and Flemish Expressionism. Returned to France in 1920 and by degrees turned thereafter to a realism that had its source in Rembrandt and was to be his style until his death.

LÉGER, FERNAND, born at Argentan (Orne) 4th February 1881, died at Gifsur-Yvette (Seine et Oise) 17th April 1955. Came to Paris in 1900, stayed at La Ruche. Adopted Cubism about 1910. Exhibited at the Galerie Kahnweiler. Dynamic period 1917–1920, static period 1921–1924, a period called 'objects in space', 1925–1930. He spent the Second World War years in the United States. Returned to Paris in 1945. His art now ran more in architectural channels (mosaics, church of the Plateau d'Assy, stained glass, church of Audincourt, decorative murals for the United Nations building in New York). Prix de peinture at the Sao Paulo Biennale, 1955. Exhibition at the Musée d'Art Moderne in 1949, followed after his death by a retrospective exhibition (1956) at the Musée des Arts Décoratifs.

LEGUEULT, RAYMOND, born in Paris 10th May 1898. Ecole des Arts Décoratifs, where he was an associate of Brianchon. Visited Spain in 1922. Teacher at the Ecole des Arts Décoratifs (1925), then at the Ecole des Beaux-Arts. One of the chief painters of *'réalité poétique'*.

LE MOAL, JEAN, born at Authon-du-Perche (Eure et Loir) 30th October 1909. Ecole des Beaux-Arts, Ecole des Arts Décoratifs and Académie Ranson, where he received instruction from Bissière and formed a close friendship with Manessier. Prix de la Critique, 1953. Exhibited at the Galerie de France.

LHOTE, ANDRÉ, born at Bordeaux 5th July 1885. Ecole des Beaux-Arts of Bordeaux. Came to Paris, where his friend Jacques Rivière wrote in support of him in the *Nouvelle Revue Française*. He painted as a Cubist. First one-man exhibition 1910. Worked for the *N.R.F.* from 1918 and wrote on the theory of painting with splendid lucidity (*Traité du paysage*, 1939; *Traité de la figure*, 1950). Teacher at the art school he opened in 1921, giving instruction to a great number of foreigners. Large-scale exhibition Musée d'Art Moderne, 1958.

LOUTREUIL, MAURICE, born at Montmirail (Sarthe) 16th March 1885, died in Paris 21st January 1925. Ecole des Beaux-Arts (1911). 1914–1915, in Italy; 1918 in Tunisia, in the South of France 1918–1919. Returned in 1920 to Paris, where he exercised a powerful influence on Caillard, Dabit and others, artists of the 'Ecole du Pré St Gervais'. Travelled in Germany in 1923 and went to Dakar. He returned ill, to die in the Broussais Hospital.

LUCE, MAXIMILIEN, born in Paris 13th March 1858, died in Paris 6th February, 1941. Pupil of Carolus Duran and friend of Pissarro. He was a Neo-Impressionist and exhibited from 1888 at the Salon des Indépendants, of which he became president on the death of his friend Signac in 1935.

MAGNELLI, ALBERTO, born in Florence 1888. Developed independently. He saw much of the Futurists in 1913 and, in course of a stay in Paris in 1914, of Apollinaire and Léger. First abstract paintings in 1915. Returned fo figurative art during 1915–1931. His so-called 'Stone period' (1931) drew him back to abstraction in 1933, a year when he finally settled in Paris. Prix de peinture at the Biennale of Sao Paulo.

MAILLOL, ARISTIDE, born at Banyuls-sur-Mer (Pyrénées Orientales) 8th December 1861, died there 24th September, 1944. Went to Paris in 1882. Ecole des Beaux-Arts. An associate of Bourdelle, Gauguin and the Nabi Group. He was then given up chiefly to painting and tapestry. It was only in 1900 that he took up sculpture. He continued to paint as well, especially towards the end of his life.

MANESSIER, ALFRED, born at Saint Ouen (Somme) 5th December 1911. Ecole des Beaux-Arts of Amiens, then of Paris; Académie Ranson, where he was taught by Bissière and became friendly with Le Moal. Took part in 1941 in the exhibition of the Jeunes Peintres de Tradition Française. Exhibited in the Galerie Drouin, then in the Galerie de France. Prix de peinture at the Biennale of Sao Paulo in 1953.

MARCHAND, ANDRÉ, born at Aix-en-Provence 10th February 1907. Came to Paris. Spent much time with Tal Coat and Gruber, painters of the *Forces Nouvelles* group. Travelled in the Sahara (1933). Prix Guillaume (1937). After the war he passed from a style influenced by Surrealism to one more exclusively concerned with painting in itself, sometimes bordering on the non-figurative. Full-scale exhibition, Galerie Charpentier, 1956.

MARCOUSSIS, real name LOUIS MARKOUS, born in Warsaw 14th November 1883, died at Cusset (Allier) 22nd November 1941. School of Fine Arts of Cracow. Came to Paris in 1903. Took up Cubism about 1911; was advised by Apollinaire to change his name to that of the village Marcoussis in the Ile de France. Volunteered for the army in 1914. Remained faithful after 1919 to a very personal version of Cubism in his paintings, in his illustrations for *Aurélia* of Nerval and especially in his painting 'fixed' on glass, in which he excelled.

MARINOT, MAURICE, born at Troyes 1882, died there 1959. Began as a painter, joining the Fauves. From 1911, gave himself up mainly to working in glass. But still continued to paint, especially in his latter years.

MARQUET, ALBERT, born at Bordeaux 27th March 1875, died in Paris 13th June, 1947. Came to Paris in 1890. Ecole des Arts Décoratifs. Later, Ecole des Beaux-Arts, where he was a pupil of Gustave Moreau, and closely associated with Matisse with whom he laid the basis of Fauvism in 1898. Travelled extensively, especially to the ports of France, Germany, Holland, Sweden, Italy etc. Settled in Algeria, but often returned to Paris, living near the Pont Neuf – his favourite *motif* in Paris.

MASSON, ANDRÉ, born at Balagny (Oise) 4th January 1896. Developed independently. Took up Surrealism in 1924. During the Second World War lived in the United States, where he had a far-reaching influence. Returned to France and settled at Aix-en-Provence in 1947. Also extremely interested in the theatre (settings for the *Tête d'Or* for Jean-Louis Barrault, 1960).

MATHIEU, GEORGES, born at Boulogne (Pas de Calais) 1921. Took a degree in English. Came to Paris in 1947. Worked for an American company. Strongly influenced by American abstract painters, Pollock and Tobey in particular. One of the chief French upholders of Tachism. Exhibited at the Galerie Rive Droite in 1954.

MATISSE, HENRI, born at Le Cateau (Nord) 31st December 1869 and died at Nice 3rd November 1954. Came late to painting. Ecole des Beaux-Arts, pupil of Gustave Moreau, close association with Marquet and with him laid the basis of Fauvism 1898. The leading spirit of the movement, but drew away from it after two expeditions to Morocco (1911 and 1912). Sombre and structural style, followed in 1917 by a relaxed and facile manner. Settled in Nice. Returned about 1927 to grandeur and boldness in his painting (murals, *La Danse*, for the Barnes Foundation, Merion 1932–3). Towards the end of his life he became interested in paper 'cut-outs', with which he did some of his masterpieces. The climax of all his experiments, completed in 1951, is the Chapel of the Dominican Convent at Vence. Laureate of the International Exhibition of Pittsburgh (1929), Prix International of painting at the Venice Biennale, 1950.

METZINGER, JEAN, born at Nantes 24th June 1883, died in Paris 1st November 1956. At first influenced by the Neo-Impressionists, then by the Fauves, before finding his true field in Cubism in 1910. With Gleizes, he became the principal expounder of its theories (*Du Cubisme*, 1912) and remained faithful to it for the rest of his life.

MIRO, JEAN, born in Spain at Montroig (Catalonia) 20th April 1893. School of Fine Arts of Barcelona. First exhibition at the Dalmau Gallery, Barcelona, 1918. Came to Paris in 1919. Took up Surrealism. Since the end of the 1939 War he has divided his time between France and Spain. Exhibited at the Galerie Maeght. Prix de gravure at the Venice Biennale in 1954.

MODIGLIANI, AMEDEO, born at Leghorn 12th July 1884, died in Paris 25th January 1920. Jewish by race. He came to Paris in 1906, where the influence of Cézanne and Negro sculpture was added to that of Siennese art of the fourteenth century and the Quattrocento Florentines. His great originality flowered about 1914. Neither the care of the dealer, Zborowski, nor the love of Jeanne Hébuterne (who committed suicide on the day of his funeral) could save him from a premature death caused by wretchedness, alcohol and drugs.

MOREAU, LUC-ALBERT, born in Paris 9th December 1882, died there 25th April 1948. Académie Julian, where he was an associate of Dunoyer de Segonzac. Académie La Palette. Wounded in 1918 but took up painting again in 1920. With Segonzac and Boussingault was one of the chief exponents of Neo-Realism.

OUDOT, ROLAND, born in Paris 23rd July 1897. Ecole des Arts Décoratifs, where he was friendly with Brianchon and Legueult. First exhibited at the Salon d'Automne in 1919. One of the chief painters of *'réalité poétique'*, so named by Gisèle d'Assailly and upheld by the Galerie Romanet, where he had a big exhibition in 1956.

PASCIN, JULIUS, real name PINCAS, born at Widdin in Bulgaria 31st March 1885, died in Paris 2nd June 1930. Jewish family of Spanish and Italian origins. To Munich about 1900, where he worked on *Simplicissimus*. Arrived in Paris in 1905. Travelled in North Africa. During 1914 War lived in the United States and acquired American citizenship. Returned to Paris 1920. Committed suicide on 'varnishing' day of a full-scale exhibition of his works, organized by the Galerie Georges Petit.

PEVSNER, ANTOINE, born at Orel, Russia 18th January 1886. School of Fine Arts of Kiev and Academy of Fine Arts of St Petersburg (1902–1910). Lived in Paris 1911 to 1915. Painted his first abstract pictures in 1913. In 1915 he joined his brother Gabo in Oslo. They returned to Russia in 1917, and in 1920 edited the *Constructivist Manifesto*. He left Russia in 1923 and settled in Paris. He gave most of his time to sculpture, but still went on with painting and theatre *décor* (*La Chatte*, 1927). French citizen in 1930. Full-scale retrospective exhibition, Musée d'Art Moderne, 1956–57.

PEYRONNET, DOMINIQUE, born at Talence (Gironde) 23rd September 1882, died in Paris 25th March 1943. A printer, and came only late to painting. Received recognition in 1937 in the Exhibition of the Maîtres populaires de la Realité.

PICABIA, FRANCIS, born in Paris 5th January 1879, died there 1st December 1953. Cuban father, French mother. Ecole des Arts Décoratifs. First paintings Impressionist. Influenced by Gauguin, he produced landscapes in crayon so summarized that they appear abstract. His first abstract water-colour, *Rubber*, was done in 1909. Cubism brought him back to realism and so did the *Section d'Or* movement, of which, with Marcel Duchamp, he was a founder. Returned to abstraction in 1913. Anticipated Dadaism in 1917 in New York, then in Barcelona. Returned to Paris and went over to Surrealism (1921). Used various styles from 1930 until the end of the Second World War. Finally he returned to abstract art.

PICASSO, PABLO, born at Malaga 25th October 1881. School of Fine Arts of Barcelona and of Madrid. Arrived in Paris in 1901. Influenced by Toulouse-Lautrec, Forain, Steinlen; 'Montmartre' style from 1901 to 1904, followed by Blue period (1904–1905), Pink period (1905–1906). In 1907, *Demoiselles d'Avignon* was his first essay in Cubism, which he created with Braque. His studio in the Bateau-Lavoir, 13, rue Ravignan, was one of its chief centres, a meeting place for Gris, Marcoussis, Herbin, Max Jacob, Apollinaire, Marie Laurencin, Salmon and the two Steins. Exhibited at the Galerie Kahnweiler. Worked for the Ballets Russes in 1917 (curtain, scenery, costumes of *Parade*). Decorative Neo-Cubism, mixed with experiments influenced by Greek art, Alexandrian and archaic. Yielded to the rising Surrealism. Brought about a union of Surrealism and Cubism to produce a kind of Expressionism that found its highest development in *Guernica* (1937) and from which derive *War* and *Peace* (1953) in a deconsecrated chapel at Vallauris (Alpes Maritimes).

PIGNON, EDOUARD, born at Marles-les-Mines (Pas de Calais) 12th February 1905. A miner. Came to Paris, worked in a factory. Evening classes at the Ecole de Dessin, Boulevard Montparnasse, where he had Wlerick for a teacher. Took part in the exhibition of the Jeunes Peintres de Tradition Française, 1914. Exhibited at the Galerie Carré, then the Galerie de France. Also works in ceramics.

PUY, JEAN, born at Roanne (Loire) 8th November 1876, died there February 1960. Studied architecture, Ecole des Beaux-Arts of Lyons. Came late to painting. Arrived in Paris; Académie Carrière, where he met Matisse and Derain. Joined the Fauves. Spent most of his life quietly in the provinces and painted in a tranquil Fauve manner.

RAVEL, DANIEL, born at Aix-en-Provence 3rd March 1915. Ecole d'Art, Grenoble, then Ecole des Arts Décoratifs, Paris (1934–1937). Was influenced by the art of Delaunay, La Fresnaye, Jacques Villon. Has exhibited at the Salon de Mai since 1946.

RETH, ALFRED, born in Budapest 29th February 1884. Took French citizenship. Came to Paris in 1905. Académie Jacques-Emile Blanche. Travelled in Italy (1906). Returned to Paris in 1907. Took up Cubism about 1910. Large-scale one-man exhibition at the *Sturm* gallery, Berlin, 1913. Joined up in 1914. After the First World War he still kept to a kind of Cubism that gradually brought him to the abstract.

ROHNER, GEORGES, born at Dijon 29th July 1913. Ecole des Beaux-Arts (pupil of Lucien Simon). Associated with Humblot and Jannot, with whom he formed the *Forces Nouvelles* movement. Work shown in 1935 at exhibition organised by Henri Héraut. On his return from captivity in 1942 he remained faithful to his very bare style, which gradually became more flexible. Exhibited at the Galerie Framond.

ROUAULT, GEORGES, born in Paris 27th May 1871, died there 13th February 1958. Artisan family. Apprenticed to a stained glass craftsman. Ecole des Arts Décoratifs, then Beaux-Arts in the class of Gustave Moreau, whose favourite pupil he became. First full-scale exhibition at Druet's, 1910. 1913 Vollard bought up the whole of his studio. Cannot be assigned to any particular school. Besides his painting, and the engraving in which he achieved some masterpieces (*Miserere*, 1917–1925, published in 1948), he became interested in ceramics about 1900, in scene-painting (*Le Fils Prodigue*), tapestry, stained glass and enamels.

ROY, PIERRE, born at Nantes 10th August 1880, died in Milan 26th September 1950. Came to Paris 1904. Ecole des Beaux-Arts and Académie Julian. He was associated with Salmon, Apollinaire and Max Jacob, then in 1920 with the Surrealists. Travelled to the United States and Hawaii in 1930 and 1935.

SCHNEIDER, GÉRARD, born at Sainte Croix (Canton de Vaud) 28th April 1896. Arrived in Paris 1916. Ecole des Arts Décoratifs and the Beaux-Arts. Came to abstract art in 1944. Exhibited at the Galerie Lydia Conti, then at the Salon de Mai (from 1947). Became a French citizen in 1948.

SÉRAPHINE, *real name* SÉRAPHINE LOUIS, born at Assy (Oise) 2nd September 1864, died in the asylum of Clermont de l'Oise 11th December, 1934. A domestic servant at Senlis, where she was discovered by Wilhelm Uhde, who launched her as an artist and helped her until 1930, when her reason became clouded.

SÉRUSIER, PAUL, born in Paris 1863, died at Morlaix 6th October 1927. Académie Julian, where he became 'student in charge', and converted to the theories of Gauguin (whom he had met at Pont-Aven in 1888) some fellow-students: Maurice Denis, Ranson, Bonnard, K. X. Roussel, Vuillard. With them he formed the Nabi group. In 1895 travelled in Germany and found the School of Beuron, the Benedictine monastery where his friend the painter Verkade had taken his vows. He found Verkade and Father Didier Lenz at Monte Cassino in 1904. Translated and published Father Didier's *Esthétique de Beuron* (1905). Teacher at the Académie Ranson in 1908. Published his *ABC de la Peinture* in 1921.

SIGNAC, PAUL, born in Paris 11th November 1863, died there 15th April 1935. Founder, with Seurat, of the Salon des Indépendants in 1889 and of Neo-Impressionism, the aesthetics of which he expounds in *D'Eugène Delacroix au Néo-Impressionisme*. Travelled widely: France, Italy, Turkey etc., seeing especially the ports, and painting them in water-colour, a medium in which he excelled. President of the Salon des Indépendants for a number of years.

SINGIER, GUSTAVE, born at Warneton (Belgium) 11th February 1909. Took French citizenship. Came to Paris in 1919. Ecole Boulle. Evening classes at the Montparnasse art schools. Was encouraged by Walch and became an associate of Manessier. Hung at the Galerie de France. One of the founders of the Salon de Mai. Also took up stage design, tapestry (Cour de Cassation), and stained glass (Convent of the Dominican Nuns at Villefranche-de-Rouergue).

SOULAGES, PIERRE, born at Rodez (Aveyron) 24th December 1919. Ecole des Beaux-Arts of Montpellier, but less influenced by the teaching there than by the engraved *menhirs* in the Rodez Museum and the Romanesque sculpture of Conques. Exhibited in the Salon de Mai, the Galerie Carré, then at the Galerie de France. Duke of Windsor Prize and Prize of Ministry of National Education of Japan in 1957, which took him to the United States and to Japan, where he was received with great acclamation.

SOUTINE, CHAÏM, born at Smilovitch, near Minsk, 1894, of a Jewish family, died in Paris 9th August 1943. School of Fine Arts of Vilno. Came to Paris in 1911. Lodged at La Ruche, where he was an associate of Chagall, Lipchitz and Blaise Cendrars. Settled at Céret in 1919. Discovered in 1923 by Dr Barnes through the dealer Zborowski, to whom Modigliani had recommended Soutine. Went to Cagnes. From 1929 onwards, divided his time between Paris and the Château de Lèves near Chartres. Few paintings after 1933.

STAËL, NICOLAS DE, born at Petrograd 5th January 1914, died at Antibes 16th March 1955. Aristocratic family who emigrated in 1919. Orphaned in 1922, and was brought up in Belgium. Académie des Beaux-Arts of Brussels. Travelled in Holland, to Paris, Spain, Italy, North Africa. Joined the Foreign Legion. Took French citizenship in 1946. At Nice in 1942. Abstract painting until 1953, then gradually drawn towards figurative painting. Hung at the Galerie Dubourg. Great success in France and abroad did not prevent him from taking his own life at 40. Large-scale retrospective exhibition at the Musée d'Art Moderne in 1956.

Szenes, Arpad, born at Budapest 1900. To Paris in 1925, where he married Marie-Hélène Vieira da Silva. In Portugal and Brazil during the Second World War. Returned to Paris in 1947. Exhibited at the Galerie Jeanne Bûcher.

Tal Coat, Pierre, born at Clohars-Carnoët (Finistère) on 12th December 1905. Military service in Paris (1924–26), then return to Brittany. Back to Paris in 1931. Took part in the *Forces Nouvelles* movement. Expressionist period (1936–1943). Settled at the Château Noir near Aix-en-Provence (1943). Exhibited at the Galerie Maeght.

Tanguy, Yves, born in Paris 5th January 1900, died at Woodbury (Conn., U.S.A.) 15th January 1954. Drawn to painting on seeing a picture by Chirico. Joined the Surrealist movement. Settled in the United States in 1939 and took American citizenship in 1948.

Utrillo, Maurice, born in Paris 26th December 1883, son of Suzanne Valadon and a man named Boissy; died at Dax 5th November 1955. Addicted to alcohol from childhood, confined at Sainte Anne in 1900. Afterwards he was compelled to paint by his mother, who hoped by this means to cure him. Produced first-rate work from the outset. Impressionist period, followed by the Montmagny period, the White period (1906–1914), the *cloisonné* period (1914–1920) and then by a period full of colour. Towards 1910 success crystallized this style. Married in 1935 the widow of the collector Pauwels, who later took up painting under the name of Lucie Valore.

Valadon, Marie Clémentine *called* Suzanne, born at Bessines (Hte Vienne) 23rd September 1867, died in Paris April, 1938. Dressmaker, trapeze artiste, and model (for Puvis de Chavannes and Renoir, among others). Her studio neighbour, Toulouse-Lautrec, discovered her drawings and showed them to Degas, who gave encouragement to his 'terrible Maria'. She was the mother of Utrillo, in 1896 married Paul Moussis, and then in 1909 the painter André Utter. Large-scale retrospective exhibition at the Musée d'Art Moderne in 1948.

Vallotton, Félix, born in Lausanne 28th December 1865, died in Paris 28th December 1925. Came to Paris in 1882. Was associated with Cottet, then with the Nabis, whose influence drew him away from an over-scrupulous realism, to which however he returned after the First World War. His engravings exercised a great influence on the movement of *Die Brücke* in Germany. Published some novels, such as *La Vie Meurtrière* (1927). Took French citizenship in 1900.

Valtat, Louis, born at Dieppe 8th August 1869, died in Paris 2nd January 1952. Académie Julian (1888), and an associate of Maillol. Spent some time in Spain (1895), Italy (1901), Algeria (1905). Exhibited with the Fauves in 1905. Eventually developed a style of more realism.

Vieira da Silva, Marie-Hélène, born in Lisbon 13th June 1908. Came to Paris in 1928. Pupil of Bourdelle, Friesz and Hayter. Married the painter Szenes. Lived in Portugal and Brazil during the Second World War. Returned to Paris. Works shown at the Galerie Jeanne Bûcher.

Villon, Gaston Duchamp, *called* Jacques, born at Damville (Eure) 31st July 1875. Elder brother of Raymond Duchamp-Villon and of Marcel Duchamp. Came to Paris in 1895. Earned his living by drawing for papers, mainly for the *Courrier*

Français. From about 1911, a follower of Cubism, of which his studio at Puteaux became a centre. Took part in the *Section d'Or* movement (1913). He had little success before 1943, a year in which his work was hung at the Galerie Carré. Prix de peinture at the Venice Biennale in 1956. The Musée d'Art Moderne held a large-scale retrospective exhibition in 1951, an example followed in 1961 by the Galerie Charpentier.

VIVIN, LOUIS, born at Hadol (Vosges) 27th July 1869, died in Paris 28th May, 1936. Spent his whole working life in the Postal and Telegraphic service, in whose art exhibition in 1889 he exhibited *Pink Flamingo.* Discovered in 1925 by Wilhelm Uhde.

VLAMINCK, MAURICE DE, born in Paris 4th April 1876, died at Rueil-la-Gadelière (Eure et Loir) 10th October 1958. He was a racing cyclist and musician and only took up painting about 1900, at first as an Expressionist. The Van Gogh Exhibition in 1901 at the Galerie Bernheim influenced him to become a colourist and made of him one of the most distinguished of the Fauves. He drifted towards Cézannism in 1908 and then, after the First World War, turned to an Expressionism that became more and more traditionalist. Published his memoirs (1929 and 1934).

VUILLARD, EDOUARD, born at Cuiseaux (Saône et Loire) 11th November 1868, died at La Baule (Loire Atlantique) 21st June 1941. Educated in Paris at the Lycée Condorcet, where he formed a friendship with Lugné Poé and K. X. Roussel, to whom he remained attached as long as he lived. Académie Julian, and joined the Nabis. First exhibition at the *Revue Blanche* in 1891. About 1900, he turned from the 'synthetic' style of his youth to a more analytical art, which was to lean increasingly towards realism as his success grew and he got more commissions for portraits of well-to-do clients. Elected a member of the Institut de France. Bequeathed a number of his works to the Musées Nationaux which exhibited them in 1942 in the Orangerie of the Tuileries.

WALCH, CHARLES, born at Thann (Haut Rhin) 4th August 1898, died in Paris 12th December 1948. Came to Paris in 1918. Ecole des Arts Décoratifs. Became an associate of Desnoyer. Earned his living by teaching drawing at the Collège Ste Croix at Neuilly. Gold Medal at the International Exhibition of 1937. The Musée d'Art Moderne retrospective exhibition in 1949.

ZACK, LÉON, born at Nijni Novğorod, Russia, 12th July 1882. Travel in Italy, Switzerland and Belgium and then in 1923 came to settle in France and acquired French citizenship. His painting was at first figurative but gradually became abstract after the First World War. Exhibited at the Galerie Massol.

ZAO-WOU-KI, born in Pekin 13th February 1920. School of Fine Arts of Hang-chow, where he became a teacher in 1941. Came to Paris in 1948, becoming a friend of poets and of painters such as Soulages and Manessier. Exhibited at the Galerie Pierre (1949–1956), the Galerie de France, and the Kootz Gallery, New York.

LIST OF ILLUSTRATIONS

Figures in italic type relate to colour plates

301

309

INDEX OF NAMES

Numbers in italics refer to the illustrations